All the
BEST
Questions!

(and some answers too)

JEREMY STEELE

beaming books
MINNEAPOLIS

First edition published 2018
Printed in USA
24 23 22 21 20 19 18   1 2 3 4 5 6 7 8

ISBN: 978-1-5064-3808-5

V63474; 9781506438085; AUG2018

Beaming Books
510 Marquette Avenue
Minneapolis, MN 55402
Beamingbooks.com

TABLE OF CONTENTS

Introduction: I might be wrong, and other essential things to know before reading this book

The following pages are full of some of the absolute best questions I have ever heard. They come from real-life teens from all different places, and I am going to do my best to offer you a basic answer for each one. But I have to tell you, I could be wrong. Some of the questions (such as "How do we know God exists?") have been asked for hundreds or thousands of years. Some of the greatest minds in history have tried their best to come up with *the* answer, yet the questions still remain.

You know what that means? It means that my answers might not be the right answers. But that's okay because that is part of the fun of learning and exploring Christianity. As you have questions and listen to answers, you are forming your own beliefs. You are deciding what things accurately describe your world and what things come up short. I honestly hope there are a couple of chapters here that you read and say, "Nope, this guy has it all wrong." I hope that because it means that you are actively engaging with your faith.

Here's the catch. If you disagree, don't just say you don't think it's right. Decide *why* you don't think it's right. Then, do some good research. I mean *real* research—not googling until you find someone who agrees with you. Talk to adults you know and trust. Talk to your pastors, ask for other good books, and build an argument against me. You have no idea how happy it would make me!

I'll be excited because I believe that good answers should do two things: help you reimagine your world, and make you think of more questions. A lot of the questions in this book are big, heady questions about the nature of God and the universe and awesome things like that. Those questions are good, but the problem is that most of the time our answers stay out of our everyday life. They stick to talking about the universe and never quite make it all the way back to our bedroom. That is why each answer in this book begins with a story from my life as a teen. I hope my stories will help you to see how these questions and their answers connect with real life.

Then, at the end of each chapter, I did my best to come up with a couple other questions to get you started because good answers make you think of more questions. I wrote a few that came to my mind when I wrote this book, but we've also left space for you to write a couple more. My questions at the end don't have answers because I want *you* to go find answers. Again, I want you to talk to the people around you, open the Bible, and begin to come up with your own answers.

I hope this book does more than offer you some answers. I hope it sparks your imagination to reach beyond these pages and discover whole worlds of ideas. I hope these words help you find new paths and discover new things about God so that you are transformed and empowered to live a life of love and faithfulness.

kay to have questions and doubts about Christianity? How
w God exists? Who created God? Are we supposed to love
s, or both? One of my family members who didn't believe in
Where are they now? What happens to people who didn't b
ortunity to learn about Jesus? Do they go to hell when the
l our sins, how can we be sure that we will get to heaven?
have questions and doubts about Christianity? How do we
ts? Who created God? Are we supposed to love God, or Jes
One of my family members who didn't believe in God died.
now? What happens to people who didn't have the oppor
n about Jesus? Do they go to hell when they die? With all
w can we be sure that we will get to heaven? Is it okay to
ns and doubts about Christianity? How do we know God ex
eated God? Are we supposed to love God, or Jesus, or both?
family members who didn't believe in God died. Where are
hat happens to people who didn't have the opportunity to
Jesus? Do they go to hell when they die? With all our sins,
be sure that we will get to heaven? Is it okay to have ques
doubts about Christianity? How do we know God exists? W
God? Are we supposed to love God, or Jesus, or both? One
members who didn't believe in God died. Where are they n
appens to people who didn't have the opportunity to learn
Do they go to hell when they die? With all our sins, how ca
re that we will get to heaven? Is it okay to have questions
about Christianity? How do we know God exists? Who cre
re we supposed to love God, or Jesus, or both? One of my f
ers who didn't believe in God died. Where are they now? W

Faith

1

Is it okay to have questions and doubts about Christianity?

The concrete was cold on my back as I lay on the floor of the planetarium. You'd think that if they were going to bring a ton of kids on a field trip and ask them to lie down to watch a video on the ceiling, they would at least put some rugs or cushions on the floor!

It didn't matter, though, because as soon as the video started, I was so drawn into it that I no longer thought about the cold floor. The video began with the night sky. Lying there looking up, I felt like I was outside at night, camping somewhere. Everywhere I looked, stars were all I could see. As the narrator started talking about constellations, each one glowed in the sky as he named it.

Then he began to talk about the universe. We started to "fly" through the night sky, seeing all kinds of amazing sights—from the planets in our solar system to other galaxies to beautiful nebulae where stars were being made to the empty blackness of everything in between. I was entranced.

After the tour of our universe, a picture of a famous scientist, Edwin Hubble, appeared as if floating in the sky. The narrator told how Hubble had made a discovery that implied that the universe was expanding, and then was proved right by another scientist. As the narrator described the beginning of the universe, the video showed everything going in reverse, on and on until the universe had shrunk down to what looked like one star. Then the narrator said this was the beginning. Everything began from an infinitely dense, infinitely hot speck that exploded in a big bang. He said that everything had come from that. After a little more explanation, the presentation was over, and I was stunned.

This video caused my very first deep question about Christianity. Its explanation for how the universe began seemed so different from what my Sunday school teachers had said that it felt like both couldn't be true. I wasn't sure what to do, and for some reason I thought that if I said anything about it, something bad would happen. Either I would get in trouble for questioning God or it would mean I wasn't really a Christian. And in the back of my mind, I was afraid that having these kinds of questions made God mad at me. So, I kept my question to myself.

Don't get me wrong—I wanted an answer. But I didn't ask anyone for help. Instead I tried to find answers on my own in articles and books at the library. Eventually I found an answer about God and the universe that made sense, but I hadn't found an answer to the bigger question: Is it okay to have doubts and questions about Christianity?

Before we go any further, let me say this clearly: it *is* absolutely okay for you to have doubts and questions about God, Jesus, Christianity, and anything else. There is nothing wrong or sinful about questions or doubts. In fact, I believe that questions and doubts are a mark of a healthy spiritual life.

Wait, what? It's healthy to have questions and doubts? Yep! Having questions and doubts means you are engaging at a deep level with your faith. It means you are using your brain to really consider things, and that's one of the best things you can do for your faith! And look, if God isn't big enough to stand up to questions, then we have real problems.

Now, let me be completely honest with you. I have been a Christian since basically forever. I studied Christianity in college and graduate school. I have written several books on the subject and have been a professional minister for longer than you have been alive (unless you're a parent or pastor or youth leader reading this). And guess what?

I have doubts and questions about my faith. I'm not talking little questions that don't really matter. I mean, I have big ones. If having questions means you aren't a good Christian, then I'm sunk.

But the reality is that if you look deeply into the life of any important Christian in history, you'll find the same thing. They all have questions and doubts too! Some of them end up with big questions that are with them to the end of their life. A bunch of them have multiple times in their life when they aren't sure they are even going to heaven.

If you have questions and doubts, you need to know that you are part of a massive group of people that includes basically any famous Christian you can name all the way back to the disciples.

Wait, the disciples? Yes! Even them! Remember the disciple named Thomas? We sometimes call him Doubting Thomas. He actually walked around with Jesus and saw Jesus raise people from the dead, watched him feed thousands with just a few loaves of bread and fish, and heard him teach every day for years. Thomas experienced all that and *still* doubted.

After Jesus died, Thomas wasn't sure if he really was who he had said he was. Thomas was heartbroken and filled with doubt. Then, when Jesus appeared to the disciples after his resurrection, we see the horrible thing that Thomas's doubts had done to him: "Now Thomas . . . , one of the Twelve, was not with the disciples when Jesus came" (John 20:24). The Bible doesn't say why Thomas wasn't there when Jesus came back, but I imagine that his doubts had made him run away from his friends, Jesus' other disciples. He had left and was alone, but after Jesus appeared, his friends reached out to him and told him that Jesus had come back. Something wonderful happened. No, Thomas didn't stop doubting. Anyone who has had real doubts knows that one story of something cool happening in a friend's life isn't usually enough to erase the uncertainty. He still doubted, but listen: "A week later [Jesus'] disciples were in the house again, and Thomas was with them" (John 20:26a). He came back!

Then Jesus appeared again. And when he did, he didn't shame Thomas or tell him that doubting was a sin. Instead of making him feel bad, Jesus just answered Thomas's doubts and then challenged him to believe.

I think this story is the best place to start when we are thinking about moments when we have questions or doubts about our faith. Far too often we allow our questions and doubts to drive us away from the church and our Christian friends. And, if I'm completely honest, some people at church aren't always the nicest when you ask hard questions or express doubts. The first thing you need to be sure to understand is that when you have doubts and questions, it doesn't mean you have to avoid going to church or talking with your Christian friends.

Sometimes we might avoid church or our Christian friends when we have questions because we don't want to mess up *their* faith. But remember what I said before: having questions isn't a bad thing. If that's true, inspiring other people to ask questions isn't a bad thing either. I truly believe that God is big enough to stand up to any question.

That means that if you have questions and doubts, the place where you *belong* is in church and with your Christian friends! I'm not saying you need to fake like you don't have any questions. Thomas didn't. He went back with the disciples, *and* he refused to believe until he had found answers.

However, the words Jesus speaks to Thomas about faith are important because they challenge Thomas—and us: "Then Jesus told [Thomas], 'Because you have seen me, you have believed; blessed are those who have not seen and yet have believed'" (John 20:29). Jesus is saying that it is okay to look for proof, as Thomas did, and then to believe because you have proof, but he is also challenging Thomas. Jesus knows that this isn't the last question Thomas will ever have, and in the future, Thomas might not be able to find a perfect answer. Jesus is saying to Thomas that even when Thomas questions and doubts, he can believe.

That's what I have discovered over my many years of questioning and doubting. Questions and doubts don't mean I can't believe. They don't mean that what I experienced about God in the past is somehow not true. Instead, my questions and doubts are a way for me to understand God better. I think I'll always have questions in one way or another, but they are a healthy and good part of my faith. As I keep looking for answers, I hold on to what I do believe and follow Jesus.

I hope that's what you will do, too, when you have questions. I hope you won't be scared, like I was after the trip to the planetarium, or run away from other followers of Jesus, like Thomas might have done. I hope you won't allow questions—no matter how big they are—to make you feel as if you can't follow Jesus. Instead, I hope you'll continue to grow in your faith *through* your questions, and to discover more about who you are and who God is along the way!

Good answers spark new questions:
- What is the biggest question you have ever had?
- What might cause some people to be kind of mean when you ask big questions about faith?

2

How do we know God exists?

I kept tripping. I was walking along a back road with no sidewalks on the edge right where the blacktop ends and the ground begins. That was always my spot when I was walking next to my dad. He was on the road, where he could protect me from oncoming cars, and I teetered beside him. My dad went for a walk every day, and whenever I had a bunch of questions, I tagged along and we talked for a couple miles.

"Dad, how do you know God is real?" I usually grilled my dad about science on these walks, but this time I had a bunch of spiritual questions.

He obviously wasn't expecting *this* question, and he was thrown off. "Well, Jeremy..." Silence. That's what happens sometimes with parents when they either don't know the answer or are afraid that if they say the wrong thing, it could mess their children up forever.

"Um, Dad?"

"I'm thinking." I could see from his face that I'd thrown him off balance. If he had been walking on the edge of the road like me, he would definitely have tripped by now. "I don't really have a great answer for that one. But I have always felt that there had to be something keeping it all together."

"Like, keeping the universe together?"

"Yeah, the universe, and people, and everything. It just feels true, you know?"

"I think so, but can we prove it like we can gravity? Is there some kind of test or something?"

"Not that I know of. Part of the whole religion thing is faith. You can get as many answers to as many questions as you can, but you can't ever really answer them all. At some point you just have to either believe in God or not, and then keep asking questions."

My dad was not a pastor or a theologian (someone who has spent a lot of time studying about God in universities and seminaries). He was a television director and producer. But he gave a pretty good answer to my question—and that answer is where I think we have to start all the answers in this book.

When we talk about God, we are talking about a being that is bigger than any human can comprehend. It's not a surprise that we have questions, and it's also not a surprise that even the smartest people have a hard time answering them. At the end of the day, we are trying to use our tiny language and tiny experience to help us understand and describe an infinite, all-powerful, all-knowing being who loves us and wants to have a relationship with us. That is difficult, to say the least.

Though I think my dad was right that you never stop asking questions and never stop trying to answer them, you have to come to a place where you decide either you can live with the imperfect answers you have or you can't. And no question is less perfectly answerable than this one.

It's not that people haven't tried. People have worked to find tests that prove or disprove the existence of God. People have tried to make airtight arguments for God's existence, but no one has succeeded in giving a provable, unquestionable answer. I think that coming to your own answer for this question is important.

My answer is different than my father's. After studying all kinds of the most famous answers to this question, I didn't find a single one that worked for me. Not one of the typical answers for this question seems like it comes close to being correct when I really think about it.

When you move away from all those classic answers and ask the people around you, some will say that you should believe because the Bible says it. Though I believe the Bible is the Word of God, that answer really doesn't help when you are trying to prove to a friend who doesn't believe in the Bible that God exists.

Other people will tell you that you can't ultimately explain the universe without having a creator. For example, they will say that even the Big Bang theory needs something to make the "bang" happen. But what happens if we are someday able to explain that moment with science? That would mean that science had explained away the need for God. That's why it's dangerous to use the gaps in science to "prove" the existence of God.

There has to be another way. For me, my proof of God's existence comes from my life. There are a handful of moments in my life when I believe I had a real, unquestionable encounter with God. Some happened at a church camp, others happened while I was walking through the woods, and others came in different relationships I had. But when I think about them honestly, I cannot deny that they happened. Those encounters with God are what hold the web of my spiritual life together.

No matter how much I doubt, no matter how deep my questioning goes, I always return to those moments and can feel as confident as I can about almost anything that those were real experiences with God.

Beginning there, I add all the other answers I have found from my life of questioning and finding answers. When I trace all the answers back to their beginning, I always end up at those real encounters with the presence of God. I ultimately believe that God exists because I have experienced God. That is the beginning. It's a place to start forming a web of beliefs about a God that I will never—at least in this world—be able to fully experience or fully understand.

I think this is the place where you need to start as well so that your journey of faith isn't teetering on the edge of tripping all the time. It's important to think back on your life and find where you think you have experienced God. As you grow, there will be seasons of doubt and questioning that threaten to suffocate your faith. Remembering those moments when you encountered God can give you a way to hold firm to belief even in the toughest storms of doubt.

Once you have an answer to this question, it gives you freedom to ask many more questions without being worried about your faith.

Good answers spark new questions:

- When do you think you might have experienced God?
- What other things do you need to think about in the same way—by asking "How do I know that they exist?"
- How do you think different characters in the Bible would answer this question?

3

Who created God?

It never stopped shocking me. In the summertime, dressed in my best khaki shorts, I would head to my Sunday school classroom filled with metal folding chairs. I would plop down on one and immediately jump up from the shock of the ice-cold metal on the back of my legs. However, standing was against the rules, so I sat back down slowly and tried to get used to the icy chair as our teacher began the lesson.

This day I was making sure I didn't get in trouble, because when our teacher ended our lesson time each week, she would ask us if we had any questions. This week I had a *big* question. I was on my best behavior all through the lesson. When the time came and Ms. Pam asked for questions, I raised my hand. "Yes, Jeremy?" She seemed surprised.

"I have a question!" I was excited. I couldn't wait for the answer.

"Okay, what is it?"

"Well, if God created everything on earth, who created God?" I leaned into the table, my legs completely frozen, and waited for an explanation to a question even my parents couldn't answer.

"Well, um, Jeremy, um, that's . . ." She trailed off, looking both surprised and confused. Then her face changed and she looked like she had suddenly remembered the right answer. "No one. No one created God. Does anyone else have a question?"

What? That just didn't make sense. I raised my hand again.

She didn't look as happy to see my hand go up the second time as she had the first. "Yes, Jeremy? Do you have another question?"

"Well, not exactly. I mean, kind of. I mean, if no one created God, then how did God begin? I mean, did he, like, *poof* there or something?"

She giggled, but then saw I was serious and got serious as she answered. "No, Jeremy. No one created God. I don't know much more than that. I just accept that on faith."

When you get right down to how we answer this question, it's not too far from what Ms. Pam said to me, though I'm going to do my best to give a little more of the reason behind it. This is a tough question, for sure, but it is a question that most people ask pretty early as they begin to think critically about the scriptures. Don't worry: there is more of an answer than "no one." However, this answer is going to make your brain stretch and think in ways you probably haven't thought before. When you're ready to stretch, read on!

Okay, we are going to begin with a really big idea in the Bible: God created everything. We're not going to go into how all that happened (there's a chapter on that later), but it's important to start with this idea. God created all the cells in your body, all the blades of grass along your street, all the water in the sea, all the gases in our atmosphere, all the planets in our solar system, all the stars in our galaxy, and everything in our universe (and maybe even other universes—see chapter 20).

But that is not *everything* that God created! There's a whole lot more to our universe than galaxies, planets, and hair cells. There are also all sorts of laws and rules that govern how everything works. There are forces such as gravity, ways in which chemicals combine inside stars, and all sorts of things you cannot see but can describe. If God created everything, that means that God created all the rules that govern all the things we can understand about our universe. Okay? Now stop, because that was a lot. Take a breath. Maybe read that paragraph again. Ready for more?

This is where things get brain-stretchy. One of the things we can't see but can experience and describe is time. If God created everything, that means God created time. Things get tricky when we start talking about time being created because we don't know anyone who has ever experienced not having time. But beyond that, most of our languages are completely bound to time. When we use a verb in English, it is in some form of past, present, or future tense. If God *created* time, then we're going to have to find a way to talk about God without all those time words. How do we even talk about something without using time? Let's try.

If God created time, it means that when we look back to whenever it is God was getting going with creation, we get to a point where there is no before. Wait, what? I meant that for real. Before God created time, there was no "before" because time hadn't been created yet. Stop. Think. Read that sentence again.

This has some pretty cool implications.

The Bible says in Romans 1:20, "For since the creation of the world God's invisible qualities—his eternal power and divine nature—have been clearly seen, being understood from what has been made, so that people are without excuse."

That also means that when you look in the mirror, you are seeing a piece of God. That's in the Bible too, by the way. Genesis 1:26-27 says, "Then God said, 'Let us make mankind in our image, in our likeness . . . ' So God created mankind in his own image, in the image of God he created them; male and female he created them."

Who created God? No one, and that means the entire universe flows from the only thing there has ever truly been: God. That means that you have within you an incredible truth, power, and beauty, because you have within you the image of God.

Good answers spark new questions:

- Being created in the image of God is a big idea. What does that say about how you live your life?

- If all of God's creation is telling us about God, what have you learned about creation that explains something about God in a new way?

4

Are we supposed to love God, or Jesus, or both?

Some people like the edge, my brother liked the middle, and I liked to be in the corner. Every night when I got into bed, I would pull up the covers and scoot all the way to the head of my bunk bed and get as close to the wall as I could without getting stuck in the crack. When I was younger, my mom would come in and say a prayer with me, but now that I was in middle school, I prayed on my own.

"Dear God, thank you for this day and for my family. I thank you for Jesus and for my friends . . ." Someone had told me that you should start your prayers with saying thanks. I still think that's a pretty good idea. "I pray that you would help me get a good grade tomorrow. Jesus, I know I didn't . . . wait, I mean God. But I know that Jesus is the same. Okay, not the same, but you know. I don't know which to say. Jesus, or God . . . I forget what I was saying. Anyway, amen."

For a long time—I mean a loooong time—I would get tripped up over who I was supposed to pray to. At this point I was just going back and forth between God and Jesus. Later, my middle school youth leader told us that the Holy Spirit was a person just like God was a person, and we should wake up every morning and say, "Good morning, Holy Spirit!" That confused me even more! I started swapping between Jesus, God, and the Holy Spirit in my prayers. All this confusion lasted until I was almost finished with college.

So, who is the person we pray to? Who is the person we should say we love and serve? God? Jesus? Or are they the same? This is a *big* question. In fact, it was one of the first big questions that the church had to figure out. Seriously, it's a super-old question. The church first made a decision on this one in the 300s!

The question is about a big idea called the Trinity. Beware! Big ideas make people do weird things. Whenever I talk about this idea, someone tries to give me some metaphor that's supposed to explain it, like the states of matter or a boiled egg. Someone even once told me that cherry pie was the perfect way to understand the Trinity. It's not.

The bad news is that I have never found a metaphor that really helped, because one of the most important parts of the Trinity is that it is a mystery. Mystery is important when we think about God. Think about it: if you could completely understand everything about God, that would mean that God was small enough to be understood by a human brain. There's definitely one thing you can say about God: God isn't small. God is bigger than us, and bigger than we can totally understand. So, what do we do? Do we give up? Nope! We are going to do our best to understand the Trinity without removing the mystery.

At the center of the Trinity is something that every human knows: relationship. Take a moment to think about all the relationships in your life. Some of those relationships are deeper than others, and over time they can grow closer and closer. If you're really lucky, you might one day have a relationship that is so close you can finish the other person's sentences. Now that you are thinking about your closest relationships, imagine you could become so close to another person that you just became a single thing. Imagine you stopped being made of different stuff and were one person made of the same stuff.

That is the Trinity! The Trinity is three unique beings that are in such a deep relationship with each other that they are actually one being. This way of explaining it isn't perfect (though it's better than cherry pie, in my opinion). It can make the Trinity too separate when, in fact, we should think of God the Father, God the Son (Jesus), and God the Holy Spirit as being of the same substance . . . *really* one being.

But since we don't ever experience that merging of two people into a single person as humans (if you do, that's not a good thing), it is helpful to imagine it as that super-deep relationship.

Now, what about the question? What does the Trinity mean when you want to know whether you are supposed to love God, or Jesus, or the Holy Spirit—or all of them at the same time? I hope that at this point you are beginning to see my answer. Since Jesus and God and the Holy Spirit are all the same substance—since they are in such a deep relationship that they are a single being—loving one is loving the other. If you are loving Jesus, you are loving God. If you are loving the Holy Spirit, you are loving Jesus.

Bottom line? Don't freak out about this. And definitely don't let your prayers get confused because you want to be saying them to the right person! God is not devising all sorts of trick questions to try to trip you up. Just love God and you'll be good.

Good answers spark new questions:
- If God, Jesus, and the Holy Spirit are one substance, why do you think Jesus prayed to God when he was on earth?
- What does it mean when Jesus says he will send us the Holy Spirit?

5

One of my family members who didn't believe in God died. Where are they now?

Susan, one of my closest friends, hadn't shown up for school in days. When I called her, she didn't answer, and I was getting worried. Last night her best friend, Rebecca, called me and told me that Susan's grandfather had died. Susan was really having a hard time. She needed to talk to me tomorrow when she came to school, and she wanted to know if I would meet her in the parking lot.

That's where I was. Standing in the parking lot across from the school waiting for Susan to get there. When she did, she looked like her backpack had an extra hundred pounds of books in it. She was bent over from the weight of her grief. Then she looked up and seemed less sad when she saw me waiting there.

"Hey, Susan," I said with a cautious tone, the way you do when you know someone is sad and you aren't sure if they need a hug, a joke, or just someone to listen.

"Hey, can I ask you something?"

"Sure."

"Okay. You know my grandfather died." She stopped for a second so that she wouldn't break down in the parking lot. "I don't know how to say this, but . . ." Again, more emotion was right behind her eyes. "He . . . wasn't a Christian. I mean, he was a good person, but he wasn't a Christian. Last year after we went to see that speaker at Rob's church, I went over to his house and asked him if he knew Jesus because I wanted him to go to heaven. But he said no. He said that he didn't really have a problem with Jesus, but he thought most Christians were hypocrites. I tried to talk him out of it, but he said he loved me very much but wasn't going to change his mind."

Wow. I knew exactly what was coming next. I knew the question she was going to ask. Susan always treated me like a minister because I had told her I wanted to do that as my career. I didn't even have time to think before she asked me the question that was causing her so much pain.

"Jeremy, do you think my grandfather is in hell? I mean, that's what that preacher said at Rob's church, right? Everybody who isn't a Christian . . ." She couldn't hold the tears back any longer. She completely fell apart in the school parking lot. She sank to the ground, her legs crossed, shaking with every sob. I sat next to her and put an arm around her while she grieved.

She was right about one thing: the preacher at Rob's church *would* have said that her grandfather was going to hell. In fact, he talked about hell a lot, then encouraged everyone to say a four-sentence prayer that was supposed to get us all into heaven. He even got graphic when he described hell, talking about people feeling themselves burn alive forever. It was scary.

Looking at my friend there, I knew one thing for sure: I was not qualified to answer her question. And I discovered a powerful truth that day that has stuck with me ever since. I am sure I didn't say it perfectly, but what I tried to tell her was, "Susan, I don't know where your grandfather is. But I know that I don't get to decide who goes to heaven or not. Only God gets to do that."

My answer hasn't changed a whole lot since Susan asked me that question in the parking lot. It hasn't changed because the more I've studied the Bible and the more time I've spent with God, the more complicated the afterlife has become.

Let's start with the Bible, and with hell. Our idea of hell as a place where people burn comes from a handful of verses in the Bible. If you read many of those verses in the language the Bible was originally written in, you'll see a word that is sometimes translated as *Gehenna* in English. *Gehenna* was a real place in that time and place. It was a place where people burned trash. It was an awful place where animals fought over scraps of discarded, rotting food. It was a place that was unclean physically and was also considered unclean spiritually. It was basically the worst place a Jewish person in Jesus' time could imagine.

In other places in the Bible, hell is talked about as existing in complete darkness. How can you have fire and darkness in the same place? You can't. But being in a place of complete darkness is scary and horrifying. It is not a place you want to be.

Other verses in the New Testament that people bring up when they talk about hell use another word: *Hades.* If you have ever studied Greek mythology in school, you most likely have learned something about this place. It's the realm of the dead. But it is very different from the way we tend to think about hell. In the myths about Hades, there are all kinds of places: places of punishment for bad people, as well as some good places for good people.

That's the New Testament. In the Old Testament, the word most often associated with hell is *Sheol.* It is also a specific place. In those times, people thought the world was flat and was sitting on top of a place filled with water and darkness. This dark, watery place was Sheol, and it symbolized chaos and unpredictability. It was basically everything that God was not.

Those are the ideas behind the passages in the Bible that people use when they talk about hell. None of those ideas are new. They all use things people knew or believed to talk about what happens when we die, especially when we have not lived a life of obedience to God. They are symbolic. Don't get me wrong. I am not saying that hell is not real or that people don't go there when they die. What I am saying is that these verses aren't trying to give us specifics about hell. They are trying to tell us something more important: you don't want to go there. There does seem to be one detail from the Bible that should be clear about hell: God is not there.

What about heaven? When we read what the Bible says about heaven, it has the same kind of symbolic language. Let's look at one passage. The most popular bit of heaven trivia people like to talk about is that the streets in heaven are made of gold. That comes from Revelation 21. What does that mean? Is the writer of Revelation saying that in heaven the streets are actually made of the element that has 79 electrons, 79 protons, and 118 neutrons? (That's what the element gold is made of on earth.) Probably not. What the verse is communicating is something far bigger. It is saying that heaven is so good that the thing that is of most value on earth (gold) is what paves the streets. If gold is what paves the streets, imagine how much *more* amazing everything else must be!

The main point of that whole chapter is actually closer to the beginning, in verse 3, which says, "Look! God's dwelling place is now among the people." That is the one thing we know for sure about heaven: God is there.

That is why a super-smart guy named Saint Augustine said that heaven is where we are fully present with God. It is the ultimate reward. On the other hand, hell is where God is completely absent. If you add what the Bible says to that, you might say heaven is really good and you want to be there, while hell is very bad and you don't want to be there.

But what about Susan's grandfather? That's going to take a little more thinking. Let's explore what Jesus says. Two of my favorite passages about the afterlife come from the book of Matthew. The first one is at the end of the Sermon on the Mount in verses 7:21-23, where Jesus says:

Not everyone who says to me, "Lord, Lord," will enter the kingdom of heaven, but only the one who does the will of my Father who is in heaven. Many will say to me on that day, "Lord, Lord, did we not prophesy in your name and in your name drive out demons and in your name perform many miracles?" Then I will tell them plainly, "I never knew you. Away from me, you evildoers!"

This is super surprising! I'm going to go out on a limb and say that most people would think that those people who did miracles and prophesied as followers of Christ would totally be in heaven. But Jesus is like, "Nope. Next?"

Let's look at another passage. It's a bit longer. It's in Matthew 25. It begins with Jesus saying that God will separate everyone into two groups. Jesus goes on to say:

Then the King will say to those on his right, "Come, you who are blessed by my Father; take your inheritance, the kingdom prepared for you since the creation of the world. For I was hungry and you gave me something to eat, I was thirsty and you gave me something to drink, I was a stranger and you invited me in, I needed clothes and you clothed me, I was sick and you looked after me, I was in prison and you came to visit me."

Then the righteous will answer him, "Lord, when did we see you hungry and feed you, or thirsty and give you something to drink? When did we see you a stranger and invite you in, or needing clothes and clothe you? When did we see you sick or in prison and go to visit you?"

The King will reply, "Truly I tell you, whatever you did for one of the least of these brothers and sisters of mine, you did for me." (vv. 34-40)

———————————

Then the King turns to the other group and says that they *didn't* do all those things. They reply in the same way, asking when they didn't give him water or clothes, and God says, "Truly I tell you, whatever you did not do for one of the least of these, you did not do for me" (v. 45).

What does this all mean? It means we are in for a surprise when it comes to heaven. There will clearly be people we think should be there who won't be there, and there will be people we don't think should be there who are. But the biggest message is this: God decides. No pastor or church leader or Christian friend in a parking lot can tell you who will be in heaven.

I think that all of this fuzziness about heaven and hell says something much more important to us. It helps us understand where we should spend our time. My wife was talking to a Jewish rabbi one day and asked him what the Jewish people thought about heaven and hell. His response was as simple as it was profound. He said, "We believe that if God wanted us to focus on heaven and hell, he would have told us more about it." True. Heaven is good because God is there, and we should want to be there, but God wants us to focus on the here and now.

If you don't know whether or not a certain loved one of yours will be in heaven, don't let that worry make you miss out on living this life to the fullest. Don't let it keep you from following Jesus wherever you are. Know that God loves your loved one even more than you ever could, and that God is the one who will ultimately decide what happens to them—and to you—in the afterlife.

Go and honor your loved one's life by living out all the good they showed and by learning from their mistakes. Follow Jesus and feed the hungry, clothe the naked, and live a life filled with the love that Jesus showed us all when he died on the cross.

Good answers spark new questions:

- Why do you think people in churches spend so much time thinking about the afterlife?

- Who are you most interested in meeting in heaven?

- Why do you think the Bible doesn't spend much time on details about what happens when we die?

6

What happens to people who didn't have the opportunity to learn about Jesus? Do they go to hell when they die?

One day, we had a missionary speak to us at school. Her name was Sarah, and I was beyond excited because they announced that she would be coming to lunch in the cafeteria afterward. I knew exactly what I was going to do. I had a question that none of my Sunday school teachers had ever been able to really answer well.

When I walked into the cafeteria, she was there sitting at a table with only one other person! I couldn't believe that *everyone* wasn't sitting there. Their loss, I thought. I got my food and sat down, listening to the conversation that was already going on. Melissa was sitting across from Sarah, talking about how she was thinking she might become a foreign missionary.

Luckily, Melissa got called to go do something before the end of lunch, which meant that I now had the missionary all to myself!

"So, Jeremy, what's on your mind today?" She remembered my name just from my saying hello when I sat down!

"Well, I have a question that I figured you had to have thought about. I wanted to hear what you thought."

"Sure, Jeremy. What's the question?"

"Well, I know that you said you were the first Christian that many of the people in the villages around where you were working had ever met."

"Yes, for some of them I was the first person to tell them about Jesus, and the first person to show them the Bible."

"That is so cool! But what about before that?"

"Before I came?"

"Yes. What happened to all the people who lived in that area before you showed up? When they died, did they go to hell because they didn't believe in Jesus? I mean, God doesn't seem very loving if they did."

"You're right. A god who sent people to hell for not knowing something that they had never had the chance to learn would be pretty evil." I was so relieved. That was *exactly* what I thought! What she began to teach me absolutely dealt with all my fears and questions, and didn't compromise on God being loving or on Jesus' sacrifice for our sins. Don't get me wrong—this question is one that has been struggled with for years. It's not simple, and people continue to try to work through the answer.

When you ask a room of kids in Sunday school how God speaks to us, you'll probably hear them say something like through the Bible or prayer, or as a still, small voice inside them. But the Bible also reveals that God is always speaking to us and to everyone in another way.

The place it is explained most clearly is in Romans 1:20: "For since the creation of the world God's invisible qualities—his eternal power and divine nature—have been clearly seen, being understood from what has been made, so that people are without excuse."

What happens to people who didn't have the opportunity to learn about Jesus? Do they go to hell when they die?

33

What does that mean? I like to say that creation is God's autobiography. Whenever we've seen a sunrise or smelled a fragrant flower or held a tiny baby, we have heard God speaking to us. Huh? That sounds pretty weird, right? Let me explain. The Bible says that God's mercies are new every morning. It's true! We have all experienced this through the sunrise. You know when you have had a hard day, go to sleep, and wake up the next morning? A lot of times, the new morning feels like you get a new start. There is some new hope because it's a new day.

How about holding a baby? You may have never held a baby, but it works with anything small and dependent, like a puppy or kitten. The Bible is full of verses about depending on God. In Psalm 23 God is called our shepherd. In Proverbs 3 we are told to trust in the Lord with all our heart and not to lean on our own understanding. Over and over again, the Bible says we need to depend on God. That is what we feel when we hold a little baby or a kitten or puppy. We feel their dependence. We see that they cannot make it by themselves. They need our help. That's how God feels toward us. God is our everlasting, perfectly loving Creator who reaches out to help us and guide us as a parent does for a baby.

Whether it's through holding a puppy or seeing the sunrise or something else, everyone has heard the message of God. Therefore, the first step in answering the question I asked the missionary that day is to recognize that there's no one who hasn't heard God's voice in some way. Everyone who has lived on earth has been experiencing God's autobiography every day of their life through God's creation.

But how does God deal with it if they haven't specifically heard what is in the Bible? There is a simple answer to this question that is very old. This answer goes back to the early days of the church. If you think about it, for the first several centuries that the church was around, there were very few people on earth who had ever heard about Jesus. Those Christians had to figure this question out quickly; otherwise, they were serving a God who was sending, like, 99 percent of people to hell.

34

What happens to people who didn't have the opportunity to learn about Jesus? Do they go to hell when they die?

My favorite way of understanding this comes from a preacher in the 1700s named John Wesley. He said that people are only responsible for the light they have received. If all you ever knew of God was sunsets and babies, God would hold you accountable for living out what you have understood through those things. The more you know about God, the more you will be responsible for putting your knowledge into action.

That helps, right? Without that understanding, God seems to be some sort of mean bully. Trying to say that God is just, while you also believe that for a *long* time God was sending the majority of the world to hell, is pretty awful. On the other hand, once we see that God speaks to everyone and that God only asks us to believe and practice what we know, we see a God who is good and just.

What I love most about all of it is the end of the Romans verse we read at the beginning of this chapter: "... so that people are without excuse." Isn't that wonderful?! No one can ever say that they have not heard God. No one can ever say that they have not seen or experienced God. God loves every person so much that God declares the biggest truths through the star-filled sky and the germination of seeds.

Good answers spark new questions:
- What truths have you learned from creation?
- What if people have a bad experience with the first person who tells them about God? Does that change anything?

What happens to people who didn't have the opportunity to learn about Jesus? Do they go to hell when they die?

35

7

With all our sins, how can we be sure that we will get to heaven?

I was walking up to a cage-enclosed seat big enough for two people. If you didn't know what it was, you'd think it was some sort of medieval torture chamber. Attached to each side of the cage were two huge bungee cords. This was a reverse-bungee. Once we were all strapped in, the cords would be stretched tight, the clamp holding the cage to the ground would be released, and we would soar ten stories into the air.

My friend and I walked up, sat down, and put on our seat belts as the safety bar was locked in place in front of us. As soon as the operator checked that it was all properly clicked in and locked down, he hit the huge red button that started the slow, loud wenches that were stretching the bungee cords.

That's when the evangelist who had been standing behind the ride operator stepped up to our cage, as the droning of the wenches made my heart beat faster and faster. "Hi! My name is Ben. What are your names?"

"Jeremy," I said.

"Aaron," my friend said after he gave me a *What is going on?* look.

"We have the safest equipment around. It's checked every day and inspected each month, but what if something went wrong and you died tonight?"

Wait. What? Did he just say that? I looked over at the bungee cords on the other side of the cage, inches to my right. That didn't help. All I could see now were the tiny imperfections: the pieces of bungee that were slightly frayed, the bits of rust peeking out from a fresh coat of paint, and the way everything seemed to rattle like a dining room chair that had seen better days.

The evangelist had paused for effect, but he got back to it. "Do you know where you would go if that happened?"

"Yes," I said, hoping that it would make this go quicker.

"Where is that? Where would you go?"

"Heaven?" I thought that was the right answer, but I was starting to freak out because the wench had stopped. Was something wrong? Had it broken? Wasn't this guy standing way too close to be safe?

"Are you sure? You know, our sins separate us from God and . . ."

I knew it was rude as I did it, but I couldn't last another second in this state. I interrupted. "I'm sure. We're Christians."

"Praise God. I guess I'll see you in heaven one way or the other."

I was just about to think that this couldn't be good for business when he ran out of the way and a loud CLANK signaled the release of the clamp and Aaron and I flew up in the air screaming like little boys.

All that night I couldn't get his question out of my head. I have always had doubts about my faith, and this fed right into those doubts. How on earth could I think I was going to heaven? I was not good enough to get there. I began to think I had lied about being sure, which, to my mind, made everything worse.

How do you really *know* that you're saved? It begins by understanding the Bible and ends with prayer and waiting.

The first question we have to answer is, What makes someone go to heaven in the first place? This is tricky because it seems that something this important should require us to do something complicated and difficult. When we look at the Bible, it becomes clear that getting saved does require something that is difficult, but the beginning of the whole process isn't complicated at all.

When you read the story of Jesus in Matthew, Mark, Luke, John, and some of Acts, you find him saying the same thing over and over again. He looks at people who are religious and not, wealthy and not, and says the same thing to them all: "Follow me." That's it. If you want to go to heaven, you have to do one thing: follow Jesus.

That's simple, but it's not easy. For one thing, it means that an important part of being a Christian is knowing who Jesus was and is, because if you don't know that, you won't know how to follow him. We usually begin following Jesus by recognizing that we have sinned, and asking Jesus to forgive our sins. Then we commit to letting go of controlling our life and instead say that we will follow Jesus. We will let *him* lead our life.

That's a big step, but it's just the first step. From that point forward, it is a continual process of listening to the Holy Spirit and following wherever Jesus leads us. When we do that, when we follow Jesus, we get the gift of eternal life with God. Do we still sin? Yes! And whenever we sin, we ask for forgiveness and do our best to live differently after that.

All of this can be a lot, and if we aren't careful, we can get ourselves worked up and obsessing over heaven and hell as if God is some kind of teacher giving a pop quiz full of trick questions. God isn't like that. When you really dig into the Bible, you discover an important, overriding truth about God: God loves you.

That love isn't based on what you have or haven't done. It isn't based on the number of people you have talked to about your faith or whether or not you have a problem with bad language. God loves you because God created you. There is nothing you can do that will make God love you any less or any more.

So, don't be so afraid about heaven and hell. Instead, focus on Jesus' call: "Follow me." The life of faith is not about outsmarting trick questions about the afterlife. It's about following Jesus. Every time you start looking to what happens after you die, circle back to where you are right now. Instead of worrying about the afterlife, focus your heart and soul on following Jesus, and you'll be okay.

Good answers spark new questions:
- Why do you think not being sure about heaven causes people to give up on faith sometimes?
- When have you experienced God?

Sin and Suffering

PART 2

8

Why did God put an option of sinning in our lives? Why didn't God make us so we wouldn't fall into temptation?

My mom was looking at me with a combination of anger and exhaustion. We had been fighting for a long time, and I was now about to be late to school. As usual, it was over something small: brushing my teeth.

I can't remember why I disliked it so much, but every morning I woke up dreading brushing my teeth. This morning was no different, except for what my mom said as we walked to the car. "I am not going to fight about brushing your teeth anymore."

"Huh?" I was surprised that my mom was giving in. "Like, I don't have to brush my teeth anymore?"

"Sure. If you don't want to, you don't have to. I'm not going to make you do it anymore."

I felt like there must have been some trick, but I wasn't going to push it. I figured if she decided to go back on this, I'd remind her that she had promised, and we'd just fight again, as usual.

The next morning, I got up, and she never mentioned brushing my teeth. And . . . wait for it . . . I *didn't!* I walked straight out the front door without ever even looking at my toothbrush. This was going to be amazing! I went all day at school, had dinner, and didn't brush my teeth before bed.

The next morning came and I didn't even think about brushing my teeth. I went to school and was hanging out with John on the P.E. field before school when Ashley walked up. I had been trying to figure out how to talk to her for weeks. She was a dream come true, and I couldn't believe *she* was talking to *me*. Then everything exploded. When I responded to her, she made a grossed-out face and said, "What did you eat for breakfast?"

I didn't know what she was talking about. "Pop-Tart," I said.

She giggled and said, "It doesn't smell like a Pop-Tart." Then she ran away.

When I turned back to John, he was laughing. I said, "What's so funny? She was so mean."

He responded, "Dude, your breath smells like something dead that my dog would roll in." Then he started laughing so hard he couldn't breathe.

That was it. I was brushing my teeth as soon as I got home.

When my mom got home and found me brushing my teeth, she asked why I'd decided to do that.

I explained the whole story, and then asked her, "Why did you let me stop brushing?"

"Because I wanted you to *want* to brush your teeth yourself."

It had worked.

I think the same sort of idea is behind why we have the option to sin. One of the key ideas in Christianity is that we have the ability to choose to do what is right. We call that *free will*. God gave us that gift when God created humanity.

But why not just give us free will without allowing us to sin? There's the problem. You can't have the ability to choose without having another choice. If God gave us the ability to choose but didn't give us any options other than what God wanted, then though we might have the *ability* to choose, we would not have the *freedom* to choose.

Therefore, when God created humans and placed them in the garden, God had to give them a choice between something bad they might want (the fruit from the tree) and obeying God. That's why God makes one rule in the garden. He tells the first human beings that they can eat anything they want except fruit from the Tree of the Knowledge of Good and Evil.

A whole lot of the truth in that story is found in the name of the tree, according to my seminary professor Sandra Richter. She explains that the real choice God is presenting Adam and Eve is, Whose knowledge of good and evil will they trust?

That story ends with them choosing to trust their own knowledge of good and evil over God's. They choose to sin. At the most basic level, that story gets repeated over and over again in each of our lives as we choose our own version of good and evil over God's. That sin is the downside of God giving us real free will.

So, why did God do that? Why did God allow people to sin? Because God wants us to have the ability to choose, and then to use that freedom to choose God. In other words, God wants us to *want* to follow and trust God's knowledge of good and evil.

There's good news: Even though we sometimes choose to follow our own desires over God's desires, God has given us a way to deal with our bad decisions. We are not doomed to have the bad breath of sin forever. Instead, God allows us to be forgiven. All we have to do is ask, and God will forgive our sins and set things right again. It's not nearly as good for us as not choosing sin in the first place, but it is an amazing second choice, and one you should choose whenever you find yourself in sin.

Good answers spark new questions:

- When you read the story of Adam and Eve choosing to sin, do you think you would do the same thing?

- Is there a way that they could have freedom and not have the choice to sin?

9

Does God really only give us as much as we can handle?

Olivia Newton Steele was the name of my first dog. After I begged for years, my parents finally took me to a friend's house to pick out a puppy, and on the way home I decided to name her after my favorite singer.

What my parents didn't know was that the breed of dog I had just chosen really should have occupied the pony category of animals, based on its full-grown size. Only when my mom called the people we had gotten the dog from to ask about food did she learn there was no way we could keep this soon-to-be horse-size pet in our average-size home.

But I had named it. I had given it the most important name I knew, and now they needed to figure out how to break the news to me. I'm not sure how they came up with the plan, but at some point, they decided it would be better to get me to *want* to get rid of the dog than to tell me I couldn't keep it. Then, after I decided of my own free will to give it up, they would take it back to the family who had already apologized, saying they thought we knew that this puppy would miracle-grow into a giant, though lovable, monster.

I remember that I was on my parents' bed when they told me about Operation Take Jeremy's Dog Away, but that's about all I can remember because of the haze of emotions I was feeling. I do recall that it involved them asking me what toy I most wanted.

"An A-Team machine gun."

This was the one category of toy I wasn't allowed to have. Absolutely no toy guns. Period. Which meant I just made guns out of sticks, but whatever.

"Is there anything else? Another toy that is not a gun?"

I could sense it in their voices. For some reason they were prepared to grant one toy request, like the fairy godmother from Cinderella granting a wish, and I was not going to budge. I would have a toy machine gun with its real machine-gun sound and clicking. "Nope. Just the A-Team machine gun."

I knew it wasn't going to happen. This rule was unbreakable, but I had no idea how far they were willing to go. Turns out I was underestimating their desperation. "Well," they said, "would you rather have it than the puppy?"

I couldn't believe my ears. They were actually opening the door to a toy gun! I was going to call their bluff. "Yep!"

"Are you sure?"

Wait a second. Were they serious? Was I about to have to decide between Olivia Newton Steele and the A-Team machine gun? I sat silently for a minute. I wasn't trying to consider which I wanted more—I wanted them both—but I had been trying to break the no-toy-gun rule for years. I decided to go for it. "Yep. I'd rather have the A-Team gun."

"Okay. We'll go get it after school."

And that was that. After school we went to get my A-Team gun, and I ran through the house into the backyard shooting everything in sight. I didn't even notice that no one reminded me to keep the door shut and not let the dog out. I played for about twenty minutes until it dawned on me: Olivia Newton Steele was gone!

I ran inside and asked them where she was. "We took her back this morning, Jeremy." What?! I burst into tears. I pleaded with them to let me get her back, but they said we couldn't. After a couple hours of me crying, they eventually explained about her size, but that didn't help.

I lay in my bunk bed weeping over the loss of my dog. My mom came in and lay down next to me, stroking my arm as I cried. She didn't say anything; she just lay there. And eventually, the tears stopped. Then the heavy breathing stopped. Then I fell asleep.

That was the worst thing that had happened to me up to that point in my third-grade life. It seems small now compared to all the other challenges I have gone through, but in that incident are all the layers of this question.

When people say that God will not give you more than you can bear, they are referencing 1 Corinthians 10:13. It says, "No temptation has overtaken you except what is common to mankind. And God is faithful; he will not let you be tempted beyond what you can bear. But when you are tempted, he will also provide a way out so that you can endure it."

I don't think that verse is saying that God will not allow you to experience things too hard for you to handle. What I think it is saying is that there is no temptation to sin (lying, bullying, etc.) that you are powerless against. You can't make an excuse like "I just *had* to lie." This verse says not only that the normal temptations of life are endurable, but that God will help us endure them. We don't have to sin.

That is very different than saying that God won't let us go through something too hard to handle. That's important because when you read the Scriptures, they are full of people going through things too hard to handle. People are killed, lose their entire families, have their jobs completely taken away from them, and endure things even worse than that. So, what's the deal?

The reality is that we live in a sinful world where people are free to do horrible things to themselves and others, and some of those things are too hard for people to handle. God doesn't promise that such things won't happen. But God makes one promise that I think is very powerful and incredibly important to remember if you ever find yourself in a difficult situation (and you will).

The promise comes to the Israelites and their new leader, Joshua. They are about to leave Moses behind and conquer the Promised Land. They are going to have a lot of hard times. They are going to lose a lot of people in battle. In short, they are guaranteed to have things happen that are more than they can handle. What does God promise the people in this moment? God says, ". . . As I was with Moses, so I will be with you; I will never leave you nor forsake you" (Joshua 1:5).

Whatever life throws at us, whatever we have to endure, we know that we don't have to do it alone. When the world seems to be crashing around us, God has promised to be with us. My experience is that, more often than not, God's presence is revealed to me in the presence of another person—like when my mom lay down beside me and gently stroked my arm as I cried. Maybe someone who knows I've been struggling with something calls or comes by or sends me an email or sits down next to me and asks how I'm doing. And in those moments when I don't want to be alone, I am not. God is with me—through another human being.

But here is another important part of all of this: Often God is present to other people through *us*. Often God uses us as the answer to someone else's prayers. God sends us to people in need who are going through more than they can handle. When you walk by a friend who is clearly having a hard time and you feel as if you need to talk to them, that is God speaking to you. When you feel that way, stop what you are doing and talk to them. Be the physical representation of the presence of God in their life. Be the answer to their prayers.

When someone gets in one of those situations that feels like more than they can bear—when they feel completely hopeless and alone—in the most extreme of situations, they might even choose to end their life. It's not because God caused whatever bad thing happened. It's not because you didn't do your part to help. It's just an awful thing that no one should ever have to deal with.

If you are reading this chapter having lost someone to suicide, know that God is with you. It may be hard to imagine, but God is there. God loves you, and God will see you through the grief of suicide.

And if you are reading this chapter thinking about suicide yourself—first, know that God loves you and is with you. No matter how dark things are for you right now, you are not alone. Now, put down this book, pick up a phone, and call 1-800-273-8255. There are people there who can help.

Good answers spark new questions:
- How could people think that 1 Corinthians 10:13 means God won't give you more than you can bear?
- When has God sent someone as an answer to your prayers?
- When has God used you to answer someone else's prayers?

10

Why do some people die in accidents when they are really young?

I had no idea what was waiting for me at school that day. I was in the tenth grade, and most of my classmates knew I was a Christian. I had led a prayer meeting in school once, so people also thought of me as not just a Christian but a Christian *leader*. People regularly asked me questions about the Bible or asked me to pray for them when things were going bad, but today would be different. As I returned from spring break, I would be confronted with a whole new level of spiritual leadership in my school.

When I got out of the car, the air felt sad. It wasn't filled with the normal sound of teenagers laughing and catching up after break.

Lisa met me at the gate with the bad news: Shawn had died in an accident on the way home from a party. He was driving drunk, and he'd also injured two other people. Shawn had been popular and relatively nice to everyone in our school. All the students knew him, so the sorrow was inescapable that day.

I spent every free moment that day listening to people grieve and letting them lean on my shoulder while they cried. They all posed the same heartbreaking question: Why does God allow people to die in accidents when they are so young?

Have you ever asked that question? I know I have. If you're hurting right now because someone you loved isn't here anymore, I don't think I have anything to say that will magically make you feel better. But I do have a bit of an answer that might help you process your feelings and understand where God is in your pain.

My answer begins at the beginning of the Bible, with the story of Adam and Eve. One of the most important aspects of that story is that God loved Adam and Eve so much that God wanted them to be able to choose on their own whether or not to trust and obey God.

When they chose to sin and went against what God wanted them to do, it didn't just mess up their lives, and it didn't even just mess up the lives of all the humans after them. It was much worse than that. Sin's entrance into the world made the entire world go weird. Adam and Eve's sinful choice really broke the whole world. As a result, we lost the perfection of God's creation, and now everything seems to have some element of evil in it. From tornadoes to cancer, all this evil spins out of the fact that sin thoroughly broke the world.

Why does this matter? Well, it helps us understand the roots of a lot of bad stuff in our world. In the case of Shawn, he had used his God-given free will to repeat the mistake of Adam and Eve—making a foolish, self-centered decision. He had sinned by getting drunk and getting behind the wheel of a car. That really bad choice cost him his life and physically hurt two other people. That happened because even though God wants us to choose to follow God's ways of goodness and life, we don't always do so perfectly, and when we don't, there are consequences for us and others around us. It's awful and painful, and it's the source of millions of tears.

But sometimes the accidents don't come from choices. They come from slick roads or misreading the label on medicine or being caught in a flash flood. All of that has its roots in the brokenness of the world in general. It doesn't happen because someone makes a bad choice; it is pain caused by a broken world.

I don't know what kinds of pain you have felt or caused, but I bet at some point you have thought, *It's not right. It shouldn't be this way.* But have you ever thought about how weird that thought is? I mean, everyone you have ever known or will ever know has experienced pain that results from natural evil (the broken world) or pain that comes from people's sinful choices. It is one of the most normal and universal parts of being human.

If everyone who has ever lived has experienced that kind of pain, why should we think it's somehow inherently wrong? If you think about it logically, if everyone has experienced pain and we don't have control over it, we should just think of it as the way things are.

But we don't. Whenever something awful happens, we think to ourselves, "It shouldn't be this way," or "This is not right."

I think our sense of injustice about accidents and bad choices that cause pain points to something spiritual. It indicates a longing for the way things *should* be. It is our hearts longing for the place we were meant to live: the Garden of Eden. The reason we look at a horrible accident and say "That's not right" is because it isn't. It's not right. It should be different, and though we can't express it, it is written on our hearts so deeply that every human being senses it in his or her core.

We were not made to sin. We were not made to live in a world broken by sin. We were made to live in a world where people use their freedom to follow God and where the world is not polluted by the sinful choices of generations.

I believe that when we feel wronged by a sinful choice or by a world that has been corrupted by sin, we are feeling the same thing God is feeling.

God doesn't want it to be this way either, so God has been working every day since Adam and Eve sinned to help us choose faithfulness over sinfulness. If you feel wronged by the world, don't try to ignore that feeling. Give yourself time to be sad and angry and all the other emotions. Then, use that feeling of something being wrong with the world to motivate you to act differently, and work to make earth more like how God intended it to be, rather than the mess it is because of sin. And know that when you are crying and aching for the world to be better, God is crying and aching too—and working to help you in the midst of your pain.

Good answers spark new questions:
- Why doesn't God step in and stop the worst things in our lives from happening?
- Why do some people seem to have easier lives than others?

11

Why is the idea of sex so pleasing?

The spring air was crisp as I walked to the patio in my backyard carrying my newest toy: a chemistry set. It wasn't a toy so much as a box full of scientific magic. When I had first opened the box, I couldn't believe how many chemicals came with it. Each one had a brightly colored bottle and a label with a weird name, like *Cadmium*.

My mom had made me promise to read the instructions and not make up my own experiments. I was sure it wouldn't take long before I got to the blowing-stuff-up part! But when I opened the instruction book, I was confused. The first task was putting marks on one of the test tubes to help with measurements. Then, the second task was doing the same thing to another tube. I was frustrated. Why was this thing that seemed so exciting so boring and *not*-exciting when I was following the directions?

The answer was right in front of my eyes in big, red letters: DANGER! It seemed that just about every experiment started or ended with a warning about how it was dangerous. If you didn't add the chemicals in the right order, the mixture might get too hot. If you didn't have the right amount of something, it could become too acidic. On and on.

Though this chemistry set was full of all kinds of potential, it was also full of a lot of danger.

I was just about to close the instruction book and do something else when I saw that the first experiment would change colors. Now we were getting to the good stuff! I added a couple milliliters of this, followed it with a gram of that, then watched as the water turned blue. In a second container I mixed another solution that turned out clear. But when I poured one into the other, they turned reddish purple! I couldn't believe it! It was so cool! I couldn't wait to do the next one!

I think chemistry works well as a way to think about this question about sex. I like this question because it recognizes that sex (by which I mean consensual sex—sex that both individuals are okay with) is often so pleasing that even the *idea* of sex can be pleasing! I think the fact that sex is so enjoyable that even the *thought* of it is enjoyable is a clue to one of the most important attributes of sex. This attribute is so important that without it, we can miss the point completely when we ask questions about sex.

Here it is: Sex is a *good* gift from God. Or putting it more simply, sex is good. Our culture often offers this same message. People say that sex is good because it feels good, and because it feels good, you should have sex as much as you want with whomever you want. That is not what I'm saying. However, I mean every part of that first sentence: sex is good.

Sex is good. It is good in so many ways. It is good in the sense of being holy. Sex is not just about physical pleasure. It is also a spiritual act. We can see this in Genesis when the Bible talks about sex as two people becoming one flesh. Through sharing the gift of sex, two people's spirits get wrapped up with each other in a way that bonds them to each other more tightly than any other act of love. In this way sex is good in the sense of being a holy, spiritual act. Don't get me wrong—sex is usually good in the sense of being enjoyable, but the goodness of sex stretches far beyond its physical pleasure.

Sex is a gift. If you have ever studied reproduction in biology, you know God has designed many different ways for species to reproduce. The reality is that God could have allowed human beings to reproduce without sex, but instead, God gave us this holy act that bonds us closely with the person we love. This is a powerful gift because through such a shared bond we can create children. I can tell you from experience that having children is a beautiful expression of love. When everything works right biologically, you can sit next to your spouse and hold a gift that was created through the sacred act of sex.

That's all well and good—but that doesn't really answer your question, right? I think this question assumes something more, and could be rephrased: Why is the idea of sex so pleasing when I'm not supposed to have sex yet? That's true. God has given us this incredible gift, but has also asked us to hold off on using it until we find the person we want to marry and devote ourselves to for the rest of our life. The reality is that sex can be an incredible tool to help you draw closer to another person and to God. It can result in the amazing blessing of new life coming into the world and can stretch you to experience love more deeply than you can imagine. But when sex is misused—like my chemistry set—it can cause all kinds of pain and explosions in your life and the life of whoever you have sex with. DANGER!

Since sex is designed to draw you incredibly close to another person, when that bond is broken, it hurts—a lot. When you create and break that bond over and over again with different people, it can cause all kinds of problems when you try to begin a life with the person you finally decide to marry and be with long-term. Again, it's kind of like my chemistry set: it can be a lot of fun and can show you new and beautiful things, but if you don't use it carefully, it can be dangerous. That's why God has placed boundaries around how we are to use the incredible gift of sex. And we can summarize those boundaries in a single sentence: You should only have sex with your spouse. Don't get me wrong—this gift is yours, given to you by God, but if you ignore the warning label, you could end up hurting yourself and others.

Good answers spark new questions:

· Are there other gifts that are dangerous when they are not used carefully?

History and the Bible

12

Did all the stories in the Bible really happen, or were some of them made up to teach people lessons?

"Then the stomach fills with acid and other chemicals that break down your food so that your body can get all the energy and vitamins and other things you need to live." My sixth-grade science teacher, Mr. Carson, was gesturing toward a plastic body that showed all the internal organs, but I was distracted (as usual).

The day before, at church, we'd had a lesson about Jonah and the whale. I had never thought about it until this moment, as Mr. Carson talked about the digestive system—but now I was completely puzzled: How on earth did Jonah survive? Wouldn't he have been digested in there?! I started trying to figure it out but couldn't come to a conclusion other than that he must have died or had some sort of God-magic protect him. And all of this led to an even bigger question: Did it actually happen, or was it just a story?

The next time I was at church, I asked my Sunday school teacher. "Well, Jeremy, I think it was some sort of miracle. I think God did something to Jonah or to the whale to make Jonah stay alive." Whew. Dodged a bullet on that one, right?

Then, because he was a good teacher, he pushed me to think harder. "But what if it didn't happen? What if it *was* just a story? Would that mess things up for you?" I was silent, partly because I wasn't sure and partly because I wanted him to say more about this. "There are a lot of ways that things can be true. One of those is that it literally, actually happened. But there are even deeper ways that things can be true. They can tell us about life and how we should live and who we are. They can talk about big, important things that are true even if they didn't really happen, or didn't happen in exactly that way."

It took me a while to figure out what he was saying, but something about it felt right. Over the years, I came back to this conversation several times as I sorted out my own answer to this question.

I think my Sunday school teacher's question is where we need to start with this: What if there was some discovery that proved something in the Bible to be impossible? Would that mean that the Bible was a lie? Would that mean we couldn't trust the words?

I think the answer is no. Why? Because the ultimate purpose of the Bible is to form us spiritually. That's important because if we aren't careful, we can get distracted and end up arguing about whether or not there is a species of fish big enough and with stomach acid weak enough for someone to survive inside it—and then we might hang our whole faith on the answer to that question.

That is not the purpose of Jonah. At the end of the day, the story of Jonah is meant to help us grow spiritually. That means that whenever we engage with the story, or with any other part of the Bible, we need to focus on discovering what it is saying to us about God and how we are to live spiritually in the world.

But that doesn't exactly answer your question. So, did the stuff in the Bible really happen or was it all just made up? I think a little of both. There are some bits that we are supposed to take as real events that actually happened, and some that are more fiction, or creative retelling of things that really happened.

There are a couple simple questions you can ask yourself every time you want to figure out if a particular passage or story in the Bible really happened or if it's more like a story to help people learn lessons.

1. Is this passage poetry? If you've ever read Shel Silverstein's poems or one of Shakespeare's sonnets, you know that poetry is often not intended to be taken literally. The good news is that the people who translate the Bible from the languages it was originally written in help us out. When they translate poetry, they change the way the lines are formatted. Instead of the first line of each paragraph being indented, like most paragraphs in this book, they reverse it and set the first line of each section or verse all the way to the left and set the other lines in a bit. Like this (the beginning of Psalm 23):

The LORD is my shepherd, I lack nothing.
  He makes me lie down in green pastures,
he leads me beside quiet waters,
  he refreshes my soul.

When the Bible indents the second line, it's a sign: you're reading poetry.

2. Is this story a parable? When Jesus teaches, he often talks about things like shepherds and sheep and gardens; however, he isn't talking about an actual shepherd, or actual sheep, or actual gardens. He is telling stories like Aesop's fables. They are just ways to talk about bigger ideas like honesty and sacrifice.

3. Is it history? History is an in-between area. Though the writers are telling you stories of things that actually happened, the way they thought about history is different than the way we think about it. Today, our goal with history books is to recount everything that happened exactly the way it happened. But for the people who wrote the books of the Bible, the purpose of history was to convey

the bigger truth of what happened using the events that actually happened. If retelling events in a different order or changing some minor details made the big truth of the story clearer, they would do that. That means that when you are reading a book of history in the Bible (like 1 and 2 Kings), it's not especially helpful to focus on the details and compare them to other accounts of the same battles. Instead, ask: What is the big truth the writer is trying to tell me through this historical account?

4. Does it feel as if you're missing a piece of information? Sometimes you find a passage that is completely confusing. Like, you might be reading in Leviticus about how the Israelites are not supposed to wear clothing made out of two kinds of thread. Huh? Does that mean they couldn't wear a cotton/polyester blend t-shirt or robe or whatever? When confusing moments like this happen, there is often a piece of information about the original culture that will make the meaning of the passage clear. You might google it, but it's better to ask a pastor to help you find the information that makes the passage make sense.

Understanding what parts of the Bible are meant literally and what parts are more figurative is a lot of fun to learn. The main thing is not to let confusion make you stop engaging with Scripture. Instead, let any questions you have motivate you to dig deep and find the answers you need. Let your questions push you deeper into God's Word so that the words in the Bible can help you grow spiritually.

Good answers spark new questions:

- Are there reasons you should not take a certain part of the Bible literally?

- What parts of the Bible have confused you in the past? Take a look at them again and figure out if some of the rules above apply.

- How can we say that something really happened *and* that we are supposed to interpret it as a figurative story?

Did all the stories in the Bible really happen, or were some of them made up to teach people lessons?

13

What did Jesus look like?

"What do you think she looked like?" I asked. My mom gave me the "What are you talking about?" look, but I continued without explaining, as though I hadn't noticed her confusion. "I mean, do you think she was tall or short? Do you think she had happy eyes like Aunt Sandy?"

My mom was completely confused. "Jeremy, who are you talking about?"

I was talking about my birth mother. I'm adopted. The woman I thought of as my real mother—the one who didn't give birth to me but raised me my whole life—was the one across the table from me trying to figure out what on earth I was talking about.

I wasn't just asking for the fun of it or for idle curiosity. I really felt like I *needed* to know about my birth mother. I needed an image in my mind of who she was. Without a mental picture, she didn't seem real to me. She seemed like a fictional character from a book or something.

On top of that, I knew that even though Barbara, my adopted mom, was the one who had already taught me so much and would help me grow into an adult, there was some important part of me that was tied to the woman who gave birth to me and then gave me up for adoption. In one sense, these questions about my birth mother were questions about myself. They were part of my identity.

I think our questions about what Jesus looked like are the same. Of course we are curious about the details of Jesus' appearance, but I think that curiosity comes from a place of wanting to know that Jesus is *real*. He is not just another character in a story; he is a real person who looked a certain way and walked a certain way and made certain hand motions when he talked. Jesus is not like Harry Potter or Pippi Longstocking, a fictional character we can imagine in our heads any way we like. He is like Abraham Lincoln or Helen Keller. He was a real person, and knowing what he looked like makes him feel more real when we think about him.

The problem is that there weren't photographs in the first century, when Jesus lived. There were paintings, but no paintings of Jesus exist from that time. The earliest painting we have of him is on the ceiling of a catacomb (a secret underground tunnel) in Rome. It was painted around 225 and shows Jesus as a good shepherd holding a sheep on his shoulders. He is very thin, with brown hair and wearing a Roman toga-type thing, with Roman sandals on his feet. Is this what Jesus looked like?

Probably not. Okay, not just probably. He didn't look like that at all. He wasn't Roman. He was Jewish. And that's the problem with all the art that exists of Jesus. All of the old art of Jesus portrays him as looking like the people the artist knew and saw every day, rather than what a Jewish man looked like in the first century in Palestine.

However, we can still get a good idea of what Jesus looked like because we do know a lot about what Jewish men in that time looked like based on archaeological finds. In the first century, Jewish men were about 5 feet 4 inches tall and weighed about 130 pounds. Most likely, Jesus had brown or black eyes, curly black hair, olive skin, and a killer beard.

Another clue to Jesus' appearance comes from his father's profession. You may have thought that Joseph was a woodworker (carpenter), but that's not very likely. The word used for Joseph's profession in the Bible is a Greek word pronounced "tekton." That word is a more general word that meant someone who worked hard with their hands and had a specific skill. In that part of the world, such people generally built buildings, but the buildings in that part of the world weren't made of wood. They were made of stone. So it's much more likely that Jesus' dad was a stone mason rather than a woodworker.

Young Jewish boys grew up learning to do the job their father did. That means that Jesus was probably trained as a stone mason before he started his career as a rabbi. Building with stone is hard and heavy work. If you've ever met someone who does this for a living, you know that they have thick hands from picking up and holding heavy rocks, but working with rocks doesn't just build your hand muscles—it works every muscle in your body. All of this means that Jesus probably had thick, strong hands and a lot of muscles from working with stones.

We don't know a lot more than that. We don't know what his face looked like, or if he preferred to trim his beard or leave it shaggy, but we know a good bit. And all of this helps us to see Jesus as a real person. Because he *was* a real person! And that is the most profound piece of the whole thing. Jesus, the Son of God, came down to earth and lived as a real human being. He worked with stones and had big muscles and dark skin and hair. He had to put on clothes each morning and wash up at the end of a long day. He was fully human and, at the same time, fully God! We'll dive into that mystery in a couple chapters, but I hope this chapter has helped you see Jesus as a real person—just like you! Jesus experienced life like you, was tempted like you, and ultimately died just like you will one day. All because he loves you and wanted to give you the gift of eternal life.

Wow. That's pretty cool!

Good answers spark new questions:

- What other questions could you ask that would have answers that would make Jesus seem more real to you?

- What image of Jesus did you have in your head before you read this chapter? What made you think of Jesus that way?

- Why do you think artists often make Jesus look kind of like them?

14

How do we know that the stuff in the Bible really came from God and is important for us to know?

I was about to see a real battlefield where a war was fought! I was so excited! My family was on the way to visit Washington, DC, and we were stopping at a Civil War battlefield. I ripped open the door of our minivan and started running through the parking lot to the fence that was clearly the edge of the battlefield.

I could hear the echo of my parents yelling behind me—something about other cars in the parking lot and being hit—but I didn't care. I was ready to see a battlefield!

But when I got to the fence, I thought I must be at the wrong place. There was, like, one old cannon off in the distance, but other than that, this looked like any other field. Where were all the bones and trenches and flags? My dad walked up and asked me what I thought. I said, "Is this it?"

"Yes, this is the main battlefield."

"But where is all the stuff? Like the guns and bases and all that?"

"That's not here anymore."

"Then how do we know this is the place?"

My dad walked over to a sign that talked about the battle that had taken place there and started reading it to me.

"I know that sign *says* it happened here, but if there's not anything left of the battle, how do we *know?*" I protested. This was not nearly as cool as I had hoped, and I wasn't even sure it was real.

We went inside the visitors' center and talked to a park ranger. He told me that after the battle, people kept telling their children about it. They would come here over and over again, and eventually they put a marker up before all the people who had fought here had died. It went on like that until they built the park and the shop where you could buy maps of the battle and toy muskets. We bought the maps and I went out and sat on the ground, trying to imagine what it was like from the maps.

That's what it's like with really old things. Understanding where they began usually starts with a conversation about the first people who were there. That's where we have to start with this question too. Before we talk specifically about the Bible, we have to start by answering a related question: How do you know whether *anything* (a book or an idea or a feeling) is from God?

Coming from God can mean a lot of things. Sometimes we use the phrase when someone like our parents tells us things they feel God wants us to know or learn. Similarly, some people write books like this one that seek to help us grow closer to God. When one of these people tells us something that resonates with us or seems especially wise, we might say that their words "come from God." But that's different from what we mean when we say the Bible "comes from God." Most of the time, your parents and the authors of the books you read don't think of their words as being on the same level as the Bible.

Why is the Bible different? I think the strongest, clearest answer comes from 2 Timothy 3:16-17. This passage says, "All Scripture is God-breathed and is useful for teaching, rebuking, correcting and training in righteousness, so that the servant of God may be thoroughly equipped for every good work."

I really like this passage because it talks about the Bible in a very personal, intimate way. It says that Scripture is "God-breathed." Think about that metaphor. Take a breath right now and pay attention to it. It goes into the deepest parts of who you are. It gives you life. It's so much a part of you and how you live that you don't even notice it a lot of the time. That's what this verse is saying about the Bible: it comes from the deepest part of God. It is not just an idea God gave someone; rather, the words in the Bible flow out of the deepest part of who God is. Scripture is part of God, it comes from God, and through it God is revealed to humanity.

It doesn't come from God in the same way that the lessons your parents teach you come from God or even in the way the ideas in this book come from God. It is far bigger than that!

But how do we know? How can we be sure? That question is a bit harder to answer in the modern scientific age because usually when people ask it, they're wanting some sort of scientific proof. There is no experiment that will prove the Bible is really God-breathed.

But in the absence of a scientific experiment, we have another tool: history. For the almost two thousand years that we have had all the books of the New Testament, and even longer for the Old Testament, Christians have believed them to be Scripture. We talk about this more in the chapter on how the Bible came together, but it's important to note that at the earliest moments of Christianity, Christians believed that all the books in the Bible came from God in this unique, God-breathed sort of way.

But the historical evidence that the Bible came from God doesn't stop there! The first part of the Bible, the Old Testament, or the Hebrew Scriptures, existed even before Christianity was around. The messages and stories in those books were believed to have come from God for hundreds, and in some case even thousands, of years before Jesus was on the earth! It's kind of like how the people who were around during the Civil War made sure to tell others about where the important battles were fought. Short of a scientific experiment, that is some pretty solid proof to use as we build our beliefs about the Bible. It has been thought of as God's Word for thousands of years by billions of people! Pretty cool, huh?

This question also asks how we know that the Bible is important. That's a little bit easier to answer. The Bible is clearly one of the most important, influential books in all of history, if not *the* most important. It has been the best-selling book every year that we have been tracking book sales except for one. It is so consistent that best-seller lists don't even include it, because it would mean that no other book would ever be able to occupy the number one spot.

But I think the importance of the Bible goes beyond how many copies it has sold. Its words have shaped the thinking and actions of nations, world leaders, and billions of people over thousands of years, regardless of their religion. From Shakespeare to George Washington to Charles Darwin to Einstein to Dr. Martin Luther King Jr.—all were influenced by the Bible as they wrote and thought about the world.

Knowing all of this is important because the Bible is a central part of how we understand who God is. Being able to be confident that its words came from God is absolutely necessary because without that assurance, it is difficult to see the Bible's importance for our own life. But for thousands of years the words of the Bible have been just that for people: highly important. They have offered grace to people who were hurting and have been used to expose evil in all corners of the world. And that is the exciting thing—they can do the same for you! They can comfort you when you are down and help you discover causes worth fighting for.

Good answers spark new questions:

- How do we know that what people like our parents (or books like this) teach us about God is from God and is important?

- Besides the Bible, what other things are necessary to know who God is?

15

Why do Christians still obey some things the Bible says but ignore others?

It was Fire Safety Week at school and I had come home on a mission. I was going to call a family meeting so we could make a fire plan. That's what the firefighter had told us to do at school, and I was not going to disobey a firefighter! As soon as everyone was home, I asked them all to come into the family room. I took out the papers they had given us at school and began the meeting.

"We had a firefighter come to my class today and he asked how many of us had a fire plan. John and Michelle were the only ones whose families had a plan. He told us that we all needed a plan and gave us these papers to help us make a plan. The first thing we have to do is decide where we are all going to meet up if there is a fire."

My mom was looking like she was proud of me. "Where do you think it should be?"

"I think it should be at the mailbox."

"That sounds like a good place, don't you think, Tim?"

My dad chimed in, "I'll probably come get you."

The firefighter had warned us about this. "But you might not be able to, Dad. If the fire is in between us, you won't be able to come get me. I have to climb out the window."

My mom looked a little irritated. "Tim, didn't you say the latch on Jeremy's window was stuck closed?"

I answered before my dad had a chance. "It is! I tried it when I got home because the firefighter told us to make sure we could get out."

"So, what will you do if you can't open it?" Dad asked.

"I don't know." The only thing I could think of was something I wasn't allowed to do: break the window.

My dad got down on my level and said in a serious voice, "Jeremy, you aren't normally allowed to do this, but if there is a fire and you need to get out the window, I want you to throw your pet rock through the window and break it."

"Even though it's against the rules?"

"Yep. Those rules are to keep you safe. If the rules are not going to keep you safe, then they aren't working, and you have my permission to break them."

AWESOME! I almost wanted there to be a fire so I could break my window!

The Bible is like the "don't break the windows" rule in my house. The Bible is full of all kinds of rules and stories and instructions that talk about everything from how you talk to the people you love to how you prepare your food. But just like the rule in my house about breaking windows, there are times when they don't apply. Let's look at a couple of examples.

"Do not eat any meat with the blood still in it. Do not practice divination or seek omens" (Leviticus 19:26). This one seems really weird for anyone who has ever eaten a rare steak. There are a *ton* of Christians who are obviously not obeying this. But why? Just as my dad talked about the original, bigger reason behind the "no breaking windows" rule, we have to do the same thing here. What is the reason behind God telling people not to eat meat with blood still in it?

The answer for this one is a little easier to work out than for some others because there's a hint in the verse itself. The part about divination and omens is our clue. Those two words refer to the way people worshipped other gods at the time, and guess what? There was another thing they did as they worshipped other, false gods: they ate bloody meat. When you put it together, the reason behind this rule in Leviticus is not about how you like your steak cooked. It is a specific rule related to a bigger rule: God didn't want people to worship other gods.

Since we really don't have that same kind of worship going on in our culture, the specific rule doesn't apply to us, but the bigger reason behind the rule does: God doesn't want us to worship other gods. We absolutely obey that; it's just that the "other gods" now are different than they were thousands of years ago.

Let's look at one from the New Testament. "Women should remain silent in the churches. They are not allowed to speak, but must be in submission, as the law says" (1 Corinthians 14:34).

This is another rule that *tons* of Christians don't follow. I mean, have you ever been in a church and heard a woman talk? Of course you have! Why do we not follow that rule? This isn't as obvious as the other verse, though if you read the whole book of 1 Corinthians, you might be able to work it out. But to be really sure, you would need a little more research.

At the time Paul's first letter to the Corinthian church was written, there seems to have been a problem with the women in that Christian community. They were disrupting worship by interrupting the people who were leading. They hadn't been trained in Bible study, and they hadn't followed Jesus around hearing his words for themselves. Even though they didn't have the training or experience, they would argue and dispute what was being taught. The instruction in 1 Corinthians 14:34 seems to be specific to this problem. Not only that, but there are other places in the Bible that tell of women leading in the early church, and that wouldn't have been possible if they were all obeying this particular verse.

Once you uncover the reasoning behind it, you can see that the goal of the rule was to keep people from interrupting worship. That's probably still a good idea, right? Can you imagine if you stood up in the middle of the pastor's sermon in your church and said, "That's not right. You're wrong." It wouldn't go well. So, though we don't obey this rule the way they did in Corinth, we do obey it in the way that makes sense now.

How about one more? "Honor your father and your mother, as the LORD your God has commanded you, so that you may live long and that it may go well with you in the land the LORD your God is giving you" (Deuteronomy 5:16).

Now this is one we still follow, right? Well, at least it's one that most Christians would say we *should* follow, even if we sometimes mess up. What makes this different from the others? First, it's a little clearer. It's not talking about a specific situation or circumstance. Since this rule is broader, it makes it easier to see how it applies to our lives today. Second, the culture we live in is not that different in this aspect. We still grow up in families. Our fathers and mothers are still responsible for helping us learn how to live. So, we don't need to try too hard to figure out what this commandment really means; its meaning is obvious and easy to apply to our lives.

That's the key: All these years after it was written, the Bible can still help us know how to connect with God and live in the world. However, some parts of the Bible take a little more work to understand because they were instructions written to people thousands of years ago in places and cultures far from our own.

You might hear people say that "Christians obey some things and ignore others." I like to think that the Bible is like the rules we have at home. None of those rules are there to hurt us, but they only apply when following them keeps us safe. Once we understand that about the rules in our home, we know when it's okay to break them. Same with the rules in the Bible. The rules are there to help us grow closer to God. Because of that, we try to obey everything and understand that sometimes obeying looks different in America in the twenty-first century than it did in Israel or Palestine thousands of years ago.

Good answers spark new questions:

- What are some other parts of the Bible that are different today? How does that change how we follow those parts?

Other Religions and No Religion

PART 4

16

Some people say Islam is the same as Christianity— is that true?

I was a little nervous, but mostly excited, as I started out on a real adventure by myself for the first time. I was walking by myself in the Appalachian Mountains. I'd say I was hiking, but I was only fourteen and had nothing but a leather water sack I had bought at a tourist shop the day before—that, and a free trail map. I was camping with my godmother, who my parents had probably hoped wouldn't allow me to do things as dangerous as hiking alone in the Appalachians, but she was super-cool and my parents were hundreds of miles away.

I wanted to get to the famous Appalachian Trail that winds from Georgia to Maine. My map showed that it was only a mile and a half or so from a trail that started near our campsite. It looked like a straight shot on the trail map. But . . . that wasn't the case. After I had walked about three lengths of my bedroom along the trail, it forked. The fork to the left continued up the mountain, and the fork to the right looked like it went down the mountain.

I didn't remember seeing a fork in the trail earlier, so I dug out my map to see if I had missed something. Nope. It should be straight on. There were no other trails shown. Since the Appalachian Trail was at the top of the mountain and I was at the bottom, I decided to take the trail that looked like it was going up.

The fork I had chosen went up for a good long time before it started going down again. It seemed to go down forever. Somewhere in between the beginning of my walk and forever, I experienced two things at the same time: I heard the sound of a river, and I saw the unmistakable orange of a sunset sky through the trees. Actually, three things happened: I also panicked. According to my map, I was supposed to be climbing the mountain. There were no rivers anywhere close to me. But there was one. I could hear it. And I had walked for so long I couldn't imagine that I could even hope to get back before dark.

I was totally freaking out, so I figured I'd find the river and follow it, until I couldn't see anymore, and hopefully that would take me far enough to be able to hear the people cooking dinner at our campground.

I started walking. I walked and walked and walked. The whole time I walked I kept replaying the fork in the trail I had chosen. I kept thinking about how I had started in the right place but somehow ended up in a very different place than where I thought I was headed. Just as I was thinking I might have to stop because it was getting too dark, I rounded a corner and saw the place where I had begun! I was home, or at least at the campsite with my amazing godmother, who was fixing steaks. Steaks, I tell you!

Islam and Christianity are kind of the same as my experience of walking in the Appalachian Mountains. They start at the same place. Both Islam and Christianity claim the story of Abraham as an important part of their beginning.

I know you probably have Abraham's whole fourteen-chapter part of the Bible memorized (Genesis 11–25), but just in case you missed the important part, let me recap it for you:

Abraham begins his journey by leaving his hometown with his wife and going to a new place to which God is leading him. He goes because God promises him that God is going to make Abraham into a great nation. Once Abraham arrives, God promises that he will have as many descendants as there are stars in the sky.

That doesn't happen as quickly as Abraham thinks it will. After he waits a loooooong time, he talks to his wife Sarah about having a baby with another woman. Sarah agrees, and Abraham sleeps with Sarah's servant, Hagar. Hagar becomes pregnant, but God tells Abraham that this child is not the one God has promised. God says that Sarah will still become pregnant, even though she is really old—and she does!

That presents a problem. Now there are two sons, but Sarah doesn't like the fact that Abraham had a son with her servant, and Sarah is positively awful to Hagar and her son, Ishmael. Ultimately, Sarah convinces Abraham to send Hagar and Ishmael away. He gives them some water and food and sends them out into the desert. Before they reach another city, they run out of food and water, but God sends an angel to comfort Hagar and reveals a water well. That's where the story of Hagar and Ishmael ends in the Bible, but their story goes on in the scriptures of Islam, because Ishmael is celebrated as the father of the people of Islam. Though Ishmael's descendants figure into the Bible in a couple places later, the rest of the Bible is really the story of the other son: Isaac.

But that story of Abraham, Hagar and Ishmael, and Sarah and Isaac is one of the pieces people point to when they say that Islam and Christianity are the same thing. To be sure, we share an important part of our story, but that doesn't mean we are exactly the same. It does mean that when we talk about God in terms of the Old Testament, we are referring to the same being that the people of Islam are talking about when they tell the story of Ishmael.

But there is more to it than that. A really brilliant professor named Timothy Tennett explains it in terms of a sentence. There are two main parts of a sentence: the subject and the predicate. In a sense, the Abraham story links our subjects. Since we share that story with Islam, it says that we might be talking about the same being when we talk about God. However, the sentence isn't complete without a predicate.

We may both use the word *God* (the Islamic word *Allah* means "God" in Arabic), but it's what we say *about* God that really forms the truth in our religions. There, too, we find a lot of similarity. For example, we both declare that God is one. In Mark 12:29 Jesus quotes from Deuteronomy, saying, "Hear, O Israel: The Lord our God, the Lord is one." Islam has something very similar in the Quran, their scriptures: "Say, 'He is Allah, the One'" (Surah 112:1).

Yet, there are things that are central to Christianity that Islam rejects, like the fact that Jesus was God in the flesh and suffered and died on a cross to provide for the forgiveness of our sins. In addition, there are things that Islam says about God that Christianity does not accept.

Though we share the same beginning, our two religions are much more like the path I took in the Appalachians: At some point, they split up and take us to very different destinations. They are not the same.

That doesn't mean we get to be disrespectful of each other or should treat Muslims as somehow less than us. The reality is that God loves all people on earth. God loves Christians and Muslims and atheists too. God loves us because God created us. Since God asks us to be God's hands and feet on earth, it is our job to express the love of God to all the world. Though we can't say we understand God in the same way, we can say that our God loves all people and wants us to love them too.

Good answers spark new questions:
- How can you share your faith with Muslim friends while not disrespecting them? How do you do that in a loving way?
- Why are there so many other religions?

17

If Jews are God's chosen people but they don't believe in Jesus, will they still go to heaven?

I could feel the coolness of winter on my forehead as I leaned against the car window. I was trying to calm myself down. It had been a bad day at school. To top it all off, my mom had said something embarrassing when she picked me up after choir practice, and my girlfriend had heard her. My mom had said something about how I still had the cute smile I had when I was a baby. She even talked about my still having some baby fat in my cheeks. My ears were burning as we drove away.

All the difficulty of my day now had a target: my mom. I was ready to scream and cry and say all kinds of things I shouldn't. I knew if I opened my mouth I would be in *real* trouble, so I was trying to focus on how the windows helped keep winter a couple inches away from us.

My mom wasn't helping. She kept asking me what was wrong, and I kept not answering her. After what seemed like ten years in the car, we made it home. I was hoping I could get to my room without losing it.

That wasn't going to happen. As soon as we got out of the car, my mom again asked me what was wrong at the same time as she touched my shoulder. That was like a switch that turned on my mouth. I couldn't hold it in any longer, and all of the most hurtful words going through my head came out: "I WISH YOU WEREN'T MY MOM! I WISH SOMEONE ELSE HAD ADOPTED ME!"

Then I ran into my room and screamed into my pillow until my throat hurt. After the thunderstorm of emotions inside me stopped, a new feeling broke through the clouds: guilt. I felt bad about what I had said. I knew that my mom had been trying to take care of me. I knew that her hand was touching me out of love, like when she touched my head when I had a fever. I even suspected that she might not have been trying to embarrass me in front of my girlfriend. I knew what I had to do. I opened the door of my room and walked down the hall to the kitchen, where she was making something to eat.

I said, "I don't want someone else to be my mom."

"Good, because it doesn't work that way. There's nothing you can say to make me not your mom. I'm your mom forever." She paused. "But you need to keep your temper under control."

Now I was mad all over again, and I braced myself for a long conversation about my temper.

The bond between us and our parents is probably the best way for us to really understand the relationship between the Jewish people and God in the Bible. When you read the Old Testament, there are many times when the Jewish people say awful things to God and try to "run away from home," but God never lets them go. God never severs all ties with them. Even when they are being punished.

During one of those punishments, God explains it to them through the prophet Jeremiah: "I have loved you with an everlasting love; I have drawn you with unfailing kindness" (Jeremiah 31:3). Everlasting love. Nothing they can do will sever that tie. No amount of rebellion or sin will separate them from the love of God.

If Jews are God's chosen people but they don't
believe in Jesus, will they still go to heaven?

God makes several covenants with the Jewish people that highlight how committed God is to their relationship. One of the most powerful (and weirdest) happens in Genesis 15.

After God promises to give Abraham (called "Abram" at this point) as many children as there are stars in the sky, God asks him to go and get a female cow, a goat, a ram, a dove, and a young pigeon. Kind of strange, right? It's odd to us, but it wouldn't have been odd to Abraham. He would have known exactly why God was doing this: God was making a covenant with Abraham.

Abraham gets the animals, and then at God's direction, he cuts them in half and lays them out with a little path in between the halves. Eww!! It's gross to us, but again, it makes sense to Abraham. After all of that, Abraham falls asleep and wakes up to see two symbols of the presence of God pass between the pieces and come to Abraham.

What on earth does that have to do with anything? Well, when you understand it, it's actually pretty powerful. In that part of the world, when a powerful, wealthy person made a contract (or covenant) with someone less powerful or wealthy, they would have this kind of ceremony. Usually the contract was declaring that the wealthy person was about to give money or land to the less-wealthy person. Before the contract-signing ceremony, they would restate their agreement and possibly even write it down.

Then, animals would be laid out just like in this passage. The king or wealthy person would stand on one side of the bloody path between the animals, and the lower person would stand on the other side. After they stated their covenant agreement, the lower person would walk the path to the more important person. As he walked the path, it was like he was saying, "If I don't keep my end of the bargain, let what happened to these animals happen to me." Don't freak out. It wasn't literal. The person was just agreeing to be punished if he didn't do what he said he would do.

If it seems unfair, it wasn't, because often, the wealthy person would be keeping up his end of the bargain right after the agreement was made. He would hand over the money or the land or whatever. There was generally no question as to whether the wealthy person or king was going to do what he said he would. The question was whether or not the lower person would be able to keep his commitment (often to pay some sort of rent for land or repay the money that was given).

When you understand that ceremony and look back at the Abraham story, you notice that something unusual is happening. When Abraham wakes up, he sees a symbol of God's presence hovering on the other side of the path. That's what we should expect. The people who heard this back in the time of Abraham knew what was going to happen next: God was going to ask Abraham to walk through the bloody path. But that's not what happens. Instead, *God* walks the path to *Abraham!*

Remember, there was no question as to whether or not God would keep up God's end of the agreement, so what this symbolized was that if Abraham and his descendants weren't faithful, *God* would pay for it in God's body! It's kind of like God making a family-type bond. God and Abraham's descendants are family, and there's nothing the Jewish people can do now that will ever change that.

That's one of the reasons the covenant between God and the Jewish people is characterized in the Old Testament as an everlasting covenant. There's no way out of the covenant for God or the descendants of Abraham. If you're a Christian, that's where you come in. Remember, Jesus was Jewish, and it's through his radical boundary-expanding ministry that Gentiles (non-Jewish people) became part of this covenant that God made with Abraham. The book of Ephesians explains becoming part of God's family as being adopted into it. I like that.

But what about the heaven part? That answer is a little harder to give because God isn't going to allow me to choose who goes to heaven and who doesn't (which is probably a good thing). All I know is that God

If Jews are God's chosen people but they don't believe in Jesus, will they still go to heaven?

made a promise to the Jewish people, and I don't see anything in the Bible that suggests that God isn't going to keep that promise. Does that mean they go to heaven? I don't know—I'm not God. But they are still God's people and God still loves them with an everlasting love. God is on their side, so that gives me enough peace to live with a question that doesn't have a complete answer.

Good answers spark new questions:

- How can you respect your Jewish friends' faith while still telling them about your own?

- What do you think was the purpose of God making a covenant with Abraham like that?

18

How should I talk to atheists and people who don't believe in God?

I was thirteen and sitting in science class next to Charla. She and I went to church together sometimes and had gotten to be really good friends. One of the things she knew was that even at thirteen, I knew I wanted to be a pastor someday.

Right before class started, she asked if I was staying after school like I usually did on Thursdays. I was, and she seemed really excited. "Awesome! I am going to get J.R. to come talk to you!"

"Who is J.R.?"

"He's an atheist who sits next to me in art. I don't know how to answer all of his questions."

I was just about to say that I wasn't sure I could answer his questions either when the bell rang and our teacher started teaching. His lecture kept going a couple minutes after the bell, and I had to run to my next class without finishing the conversation with Charla.

As I walked out of my last class of the day and went into the little courtyard where we all hung out, I saw Charla waiting with another student who I figured had to be J.R. We introduced ourselves and started talking about faith. He had a lot of questions, and I had some answers, but what really started there was a friendship. I now had my first atheist friend.

Talking to an atheist friend isn't as hard as you might think. Over the years, for whatever reason, God has given me the gift of being the person to whom people send their friends and family members who don't believe in Jesus. If I'm completely honest, some of my favorite people to interact with are atheists, but that's another story.

When people ask me how to talk to atheists, it's usually because they have a genuine concern for someone they love dearly and are confused as to where they should start.

Where *do* you start? How do you talk about your faith without pushing the person away, fighting with them, or making your faith seem shallow?

First of all, don't argue. This is key. I don't know any atheist who has ever been convinced to be a Christian through a theological or philosophical argument with a friend or family member. The argument approach is fraught with all sorts of difficult issues. There are a couple reasons for this.

First among them is that atheists don't believe in the sources of authority Christians take for granted, such as the Bible. You can quote as many Bible verses as you want and even explain the historical reliability of the ancient texts, but it won't matter because they don't believe in God. For them, the words in the Bible are interesting philosophy, but as far as they're concerned, the Bible can't be God's Word because they don't believe God exists.

The atheists I have met are also intensely skeptical, which is something for which I personally have a deep respect. However, unless you have the same level of skepticism, you will likely be caught off guard by their questioning of basic truths and realities, and will find yourself unsure of how to respond.

Another problem with arguing with atheists is that there really isn't a perfect way to prove God exists using logical arguments. Though people have tried for centuries to create a logical proof for God, it hasn't ever worked. Don't get me wrong—many have written proofs. But all such proofs can be dismissed by a group of freshman philosophy students (trust me, I've seen it).

One of the most troubling aspects of religion to atheists is that God exists, in some part, beyond logic. That's not to say that faith is illogical, but that it talks about ultimate things and spiritual realities that extend beyond our experience and ability to explain.

Finally, there are often deeper issues that undergird their viewpoint. Like every human ever, atheists have experienced deep pain and loss. Some have been torn apart by Christians in their school, some have been shamed by Christian parents, some have watched as their children died, some have been alienated by pastors, and some have suffered even more horrific things. These sorts of trials would shake the faith of even the most devout Christian. To a person who was not all that sure about God to begin with, such hurts represent proof that this world lacks the presence of a loving God.

Though there are philosophical and theological answers to all those problems, such answers provide little comfort for the deep emotional pain and unsettling loss wrapped up in those stories. And no one—*no one*—has ever found healing from abuse or loss through a theological argument with a person of faith.

When it comes down to it, all you have is your own story. When you are interacting with a person whose beliefs are in direct contradiction with the most fundamental elements of your own, none of your theology has any validity from their perspective. When the Bible is irrelevant in the discussion, along with all the theological stances of your particular denomination, all you have left is your own experience of God in your life.

But that is a lot! Your story contains the same truth of God that exists in the Bible, but in a narrative, personal form. There is real power in our stories, because though others may not share your theological beliefs, they do share the experience of being human. You have both loved and lost and been hurt and seen beauty.

So, you share your story. In sharing how you have experienced God, you are sharing the gospel. In revealing how you deal with doubts, you give voice to the Holy Spirit. And when you talk about experiencing the transcendent presence of God in nature, you are speaking the words of God that have been written into sunsets and fields of flowers.

All of this leads me to what is possibly the most important piece. The way you talk to your atheist friends is to have a *thousand* interactions about faith, not just one. The goal is not to convert them in a single moment of evangelism, but to share the story of God in your life as often as possible.

Most people avoid talking about faith with their atheist friends because they don't want to make the other person uncomfortable. But talking about faith is only uncomfortable if you only bring it up as part of a concerted effort to argue and change their mind.

Instead of constantly trying to preach at people who don't believe in God, we need to live our faith openly and publicly so they can see the work of God in our lives. Doing that means being honest about the fact that you spent time in prayer before you got ready for the day, or how much it meant to you that your small-group leader came by the hospital and prayed with you before your surgery. It means sharing a scripture that helped you out or talking about how the evil in the world frustrates you.

And it also means letting them see you question and doubt and find an answer or live with the unknown. It means expressing when you are angry at God for allowing humans to have free will and do evil things, and offering to pray for them when things are less than good in their lives.

It means allowing the Holy Spirit to speak a thousand tiny messages of hope to them through your words and actions.

When it all comes down to it, there is really nothing we can do on our own to convert anyone to Christianity. If your friend decides to follow Jesus, it will not be because of something you said. It will be because of the Holy Spirit working in their heart. That means that in this situation, you are a tool for the Holy Spirit to use.

This is a stretching moment for most people. The question is whether or not you will trust the Holy Spirit. The answer may be no—in which case you should study all kinds of arguments against atheism and make sure to have a lot of fights with people who don't believe in God. But if you truly want the people you encounter to experience the love and power of being filled with the Spirit as they follow Jesus, you are going to have to grow in your own faith to the point that you can trust the Holy Spirit with the soul of your nonbelieving friend.

Which should lead you to your knees—because when faced with the fact that we are the vessel for the Holy Spirit, we are always confronted with our own brokenness and the need to be healed. So, pray. Pray for your friend, pray for yourself, pray for the Holy Spirit to use your story and the thousands of interactions you and your friend will have. Then trust, because at the end of the day, it's not up to you.

Good answers spark new questions:
- Why hasn't anyone come up with a way to prove God exists after thousands of years of trying?
- Why do bad things in life make some people draw closer to God and some people walk away?
- How should you respond if your atheist friend seems to be picking fights with you about God?

19

Should I be friends with people from other religions?

By the time I was in the seventh grade, I was getting really close to developing the perfect recipe for spaghetti sauce. Two years earlier, I had watched a cooking show on TV where the chef was making spaghetti sauce, and at the end they said, "Spaghetti sauce is a perfect thing for young cooks because they really can't mess it up." I looked at my mom and said, "Can I try to make spaghetti sauce from scratch like that?" She said yes, and I immediately got up from the couch to see if there was tomato sauce in the pantry.

Over the next several years I experimented with tomato sauce versus tomato paste versus diced tomatoes (only to discover that crushed tomatoes were the perfect option). And I tried all kinds of spices, from oregano to sugar (I know . . . sugar was a bad idea). Every time I would learn what spices worked and what didn't.

Now, closing in on a perfect recipe, I decided to try something different. The day before, I had watched an episode of *Dragnet* (a cop show) where one of the main characters said the secret to his barbecue sauce was adding vanilla ice cream. I thought it was weird, but everyone on the show loved the sauce, so I decided I was going to add some to my spaghetti sauce the next time I made it.

It was now the moment of truth. I had added all of my more typical spices, such as oregano and basil and pepper and thyme, and was holding in my hand my dad's quart of ice cream. I was second-guessing this choice. Even though I didn't know how it would taste, I knew one thing for sure: it would *change* the taste.

After arguing with myself for five minutes or so, I added a couple scoops. It changed the taste, and it tasted . . . different. Okay, it tasted horrible.

New friends are kind of like adding spices to spaghetti sauce. Whether we want to admit it or not, friends change who we are as they become more and more a part of our lives. So, what about friends who are from other religions? Are they a scoop of ice cream in our spaghetti sauce, or a little extra oregano?

I think that when we ask this question, we are usually responding to one or two concerns. First, some people think that the Bible says somewhere that we shouldn't associate with people of other faiths. And second, on a more personal level, people are afraid that being friends with a person of another faith might lead them away from their own faith in Jesus. Let's think about both of these concerns.

First, the Bible. To be sure, there are several places in the Old Testament where God instructs the people of Israel to not associate with other groups of people. In those verses, God implies that the other groups will lead the Israelites away from God.

In those verses, God calls the people of Israel to live very different lives as an example to the rest of the world. Their lives were to be a symbol of purity, to the point that they didn't even wear clothes sewn out of fabric made from two different types of thread. God wanted them to be distinct so that God's people stood out and the world would see both that they were different and that God blessed them for being obedient.

Keeping their families unmixed with people from the outside world was part of that same value.

However, staying away from people of other groups doesn't seem to have been a major, ongoing priority. By the time we read the lineage of Jesus at the beginning of Matthew, it is filled with people who were not Jewish. That's important to note because part of what it is saying about Jesus from the very beginning is that he came to break down the wall of separation between the Jews and the Gentiles and make a relationship with God available to all.

As far as the Bible is concerned, the choice is up to you. But what about the fear that being friends with someone of another faith will make you lose your own? That fear is legitimate, but it is based in the belief that having your faith challenged is always bad.

One of the main ideas behind this book is that God and God's Word can withstand any level of questioning. There is no question about faith that we should be afraid of. Having questions about your faith or being challenged to think deeply about your faith is a good thing. It helps you grow.

Instead of worrying that a conversation with a friend of another faith will lead you astray, I think it's better to see those conversations (and the questions that will come out of them) as opportunities to learn more about God, the Bible, and Christianity.

I guess what I'm saying is that, in a way, being friends with a person of another religion could help you grow as a Christian.

But what we are talking about here is bigger than people of other religions. Whether a person will lead you away from Jesus is always an important question to ask because I have seen people who added friends to their life and it worked just about as well as adding a scoop of ice cream to spaghetti sauce. There are many ways that your friends can cause you to walk away from Jesus, and I think the most dangerous ones have nothing to do with their religion. Their character, their habits, and the choices they make have a much bigger impact than their religion. The person they are and the direction they are headed will most certainly have an effect on your life.

So, I want you to ask yourself these question: Are my friends headed in the direction I want to be headed? When I fast-forward their habits and choices into the future, are they going to end up where I want to be? Are they going to end up where *God* wants me to be? When you answer these questions, you'll know whether or not you should be their friend. Then you can let your conversations about faith help you grow, and you can show anyone who is watching how the love of God is present in your life.

Good answers spark new questions:

- What are some things people might be doing now that could lead to bad results in the future?

- How do you end a friendship with a person who is a bad influence without being mean?

- Who do you want to be in the future?

Science and Creation

PART 5

20

Did God create other universes?

I loved acting when I was in elementary school. I was always in the plays at our church, but I played the roles of young characters in local high school and college plays too. I loved every second of it and thought that maybe one day I would move to New York and become a star on Broadway.

When I was going into the fifth grade, I had an opportunity that I thought might give me the big break I needed to become a huge star. I had auditioned for an acting camp that happened outside New York City. The final day of camp was a performance in New York City in front of a bunch of agents and managers. After a lot of talking about how we could afford it, my parents gave me the news that I was able to go. That wasn't even the best part. After camp, we would spend a couple weeks going to auditions in New York City!

It was as if my brain had been given a shot of pure imagination. I instantly saw my future landing major roles in Broadway musicals that would, of course, put me in the perfect position to begin a long and lucrative career in movies. Every time I calmed myself down, I would ramp up on another subject, such as what it would be like to live at the top of one of those New York skyscrapers or if I would be able to keep myself together when I performed for the first time on the *Today* show.

I could tell my brother wasn't sharing my excitement, so I picked up the phone and called one of my best friends who had already decided that she would move to New York with me after high school and become a professional dancer. I assured her that I would use my extensive contacts to help her get a job, and I'd let her stay with me for free because I would most certainly be a millionaire by that time.

I think a similar shot of pure imagination is at play when people think about everything God created. We barely understand our own planet, which represents a fraction of a fraction of a *fraction* of everything God made. All of that unknown begs us to dream. It calls to us to seek to understand. We spend most of our time thinking about our faith in terms of what has happened here on earth, but how does our understanding of everything else interact with our faith?

Before we go much further, it's probably helpful to bring you up to speed on the whole multiple-universes idea. As scientists seek to explain how our universe began a little over 13 billion years ago, they have begun to consider a major idea: What if there were multiple universes?

The idea put forth by Stephen Hawking and others is that entire universes are constantly being born and dying, with many lasting only fractions of a second. The idea is that each universe begins with a new set of laws and ideas that govern it (like our law of gravity). Since the majority of combinations of laws will not support a viable universe, most of them collapse. But every once in a while, the conditions are perfect, and a sustainable universe is created that grows and develops, like our own. It's a pretty incredible idea.

But where does God fit into that? For those answers we have to explore the creation story in the Bible. The problem, though, is that the creation story in the book of Genesis was written by and to a people who had no idea of quantum physics or the theory of relativity. They didn't know what we know about our universe. They didn't even know that the earth orbits around the sun!

If they didn't have even the most basic scientific understanding, how do we use information written by and to them to respond to modern science? The key is trying to enter into their mindset to understand at the most basic level what the Bible was saying to them. Then we can figure out what that might mean in the modern day.

The very beginning of the Bible gives us the most insight: "In the beginning, God created the heavens and the earth. Now the earth was formless and empty, darkness was over the surface of the deep, and the Spirit of God was hovering over the waters" (Genesis 1:1-2).

Imagine you are living long before humans knew that the earth was round. You are sitting next to a fire listening to a priest tell this story. You look up at the thousands of stars in the sky and then are told that the two biggest things you can see, the land and the sky, were created by God. What would that mean to you? I think it would say to you that *everything* was created by God because everything you have ever known was either in the sky or on the land. Every camel, every bird, every tree, and every cloud—it all existed either in land or sky. Okay, or the sea, but later in the story God creates that too.

Now, as we fast-forward several thousand years into the modern day and try to translate the deepest truth of the creation story into a world that is as familiar with the electron as with the donkey, the task is pretty simple. That basic truth makes a lot of sense even today: God created everything. God created all the atoms and planets and solar systems and galaxies, and, if it turns out to be true that there are multiple universes, all the universes too! When we read the book of Genesis we have to say that if there are other universes, God must have created them too.

If there are other universes that God created, that could lead to some significant questions about God and how God relates with us. For example, did Jesus die just for humans or for all beings everywhere? What if the beings in another universe never chose to sin like we did?

The more you think about it, the more questions you can create. It's like another one of those shots of pure imagination. To have a full answer to all of the questions, we usually need information we don't have because we haven't experienced other worlds or universes. However, the questions all seem to ask whether God relates the same with all creations or if God relates differently from one to the other.

For that, we can offer an answer. Though the relationship may be different based on the specifics of the creation, if all of these universes were created by God, then they would all be cared for by God as creator. Or, in the words of my mom, "God may love us in different ways, but the same amount."

Good answers spark new questions:

- Think about the idea of other universes. In five minutes, how many God questions does that bring up for you?

- What might be a reason that God wouldn't teach the ancient people about electrons and universes before telling them the creation story?

21

Why do scientists believe that God didn't create the earth?

My godfather was awesome. He wasn't awesome just because he let me call him Uncle Bear (that's a whole other story), but also because he was a woodworking artist. As far as I was concerned, he could make anything out of wood. Want proof? Behind his house he had built another, smaller house just for a workshop, and it was amazing.

When you walked in there, it was like entering a power-tool wonderland. There were, like, a million different kinds of drills and saws and sanders. If you wanted to hold something together, there were, like, a thousand tool options, from bar clamps to C-clamps to vice grips and even some cool wooden clamps that had two giant screws in them.

Once I asked him if we could make a puppet theater for me to do puppet shows in. He said yes, and we spent a couple hours talking about the design and making plans for it. Then a few days later, I headed over to actually work on it with him in his workshop.

I was in heaven! We would measure, mark, and cut, and then do it all again, over and over, with the loud roar of the table saw fading into the next instructions from Uncle Bear. It felt like we had just started when his wife came in and said, "Jeremy's mom just called and she's on the way to pick him up."

It was at that moment that I realized that we had only used one tool the entire time: the table saw. "Uncle Bear, can we use another saw?"

"What do you mean?"

"Well, we spent our whole time only using one tool, and I was hoping we might be able to use all of them. Especially that cool one over there with the tiny saw blade in the middle of it."

"You mean this one?" He pointed to the one I was talking about. It looked like it should have been on a spaceship. It had a tiny little square table on it with a saw blade that was smaller than a blade of grass going through it and held at the top by a long metal arm of some sort.

"Yeah. That one. The one that looks like part of a spaceship."

He laughed as he replied, "It's actually called a coping saw, and it won't work for this project."

"Why not?"

"Well, it's really good at making very curvy, very detailed cuts, but it's not good at making long straight cuts very well."

"Yeah, that would be bad for the puppet theater. What do you make with it?"

"Remember those wooden ornaments I gave your mom?"

"Yep."

"I made those with it."

"Wow! That's cool! Maybe we could make some curly things with it to add as a decoration or something."

"That would work. I'll glue all this together and we can see about adding something with the coping saw next time."

Then my mom was there and I had to leave the magical workshop so I could do my homework.

I think about my godfather's tools when I try to figure out why scientists don't believe that God created the earth. It's really all about tools.

For one reason or another, over the past couple thousand years, many church leaders have found themselves in opposition with scientists. Whether it was when scientists were first proposing that the sun was the center of the universe or when they began to suggest that the human race evolved from other species, there have always been some church leaders arguing against science.

The funny thing is that a lot of the controversial scientists in our history were actually Christians. They went to church and studied the Bible and even struggled with what their research might suggest about the teachings of the church.

I remember struggling with this same question as I was growing up. In church, sometimes grown-ups told me that scientists believed that God didn't create the earth. I thought I had to be very suspicious of my science teachers so they wouldn't make me have doubts about my faith. I eventually met a professor in college who was an evolutionary biologist and a leader in his Southern Baptist church. When I asked him about this whole thing, he gave me a very simple response.

"I actually believe that God created the earth, *and* that everything science says about the way it all started is true as well." He went on to explain that he thought of it as science and religion having different tools.

I love that answer because it makes total sense to me. On the one hand, you have the tools that come from the scientific method. These scientific tools are great at discovering how things work. They work well for finding causes and effects, and they have produced some of the most amazing things, like medicine and cars and smartphones.

On the other hand, religion has a whole other set of tools that help us understand morality and love and the purpose of life as we join God in God's mission. Religion helps us probe the deep places within our soul that cannot be explored with a microscope or an MRI. Most importantly, religion helps us understand the character of God.

What I have discovered is that these two sets of tools are not at war. As a person who loves both science and religion, I feel that when we use both sets of tools responsibly, their two perspectives can offer us beautiful insights. Where religion might tell us *why* God created the earth, science can tell us *how* God created the earth.

The problem is that when we use the wrong tool, we get awful results. Much like trying to cut straight lines with a coping saw, when we use the tools of religion to do science or the tools of science to do religion, everything looks wrong and doesn't seem to match.

That means that if we have a question about science, we can feel confident in using the tools of science to answer that question. Then, when we have a question about faith, we use the tools of religion. And we never need to feel guilty about using one or the other because God gave us both as gifts—gifts God wants us to use!

Good answers spark new questions:
- Are there other sets of tools besides science and religion?
- How do we use these tools responsibly?
- If we look at the stories in Genesis as being about *why* God created the earth, what answer do we get?

22

Did Genesis really happen? Like, is that how the earth was made?

The first time I understood a poem, it was like the door to another world opened up to me. The teacher began our lesson by asking my friend Michelle, who sat right in front of me, to read the poem "The Road Not Taken" by Robert Frost.

"Two roads diverged in a yellow wood, and sorry I could not travel both . . ." Michelle's voice was loud enough to almost echo off the four cinderblock walls coated in thirty years' worth of paint.

It seemed like a straightforward story of a man walking in the woods. Then our teacher got up and asked what we thought the poem was about. No one said anything, so I responded, "It's about a guy going on a walk in the woods."

"Yes. That is what it's about, but what *else* is it about?" The way she said the word *else* made me think she was about to reveal a secret of the universe or something.

For me, that's exactly what she did. Over the next couple minutes, she talked about how the poem had layers of truth. Most people feel that it encourages them to not follow the crowd, but to take the road less traveled. Some have argued that the poem is really about how we always regret decisions in our past.

Then the teacher read it again and asked us to listen to it speak to us about something deeper. When it came to the final stanza and she read, "Two roads diverged in a wood and I—I took the one less traveled by, and that has made all the difference," it hit me like a wave: how all the little choices we make ultimately direct our lives.

It's hard for me to express how much of an impact that day in class had on me. I felt like my mind had been opened to a new level of thinking. I had seen that sometimes there are deep truths just below the surface of words, and I couldn't wait to get home and see what other poetry I could find.

I had a similar experience in another class while studying the book of Genesis. If I am honest, the beginning of Genesis had bothered me for a long time because of how it seemed to conflict with science. I remember wondering, Is that really how the earth was made, or was it the way all my science textbooks said?

I had thought about it and studied it for a long time without finding any way for the two explanations of the beginning of the world to agree. All of that was about to change. My professor walked into the room and asked one of us to read from Genesis 1, and after a couple of verses he interrupted and said, "What kind of literature is this?" No one answered. "Is it a science textbook? Is it a legal code?" More silence.

He then asked us to look carefully at the lines in our Bible. He said that the translators of the scripture are giving us clues about the text by how they put it on the page.

He was right. I'd never noticed it before, but the first chapter of Genesis has all kinds of breaks in the lines. It looked like a poem. (More on that in chapter 12) He asked where else we had seen text in the Bible spaced like that, to which one of my classmates blurted out, "Psalms!"

"That's right!" the professor said with that smirk teachers get when they see their students understanding a new concept.

"So," another student began tentatively, "are you saying that this is a poem?"

"Yes, but it's not just any poem. It is a deep piece of philosophical poetry that is so profound and well developed that it is really a marvel of the ancient world."

When you grasp this fact about the beginning of Genesis, it really helps you discover some incredible truths. You realize that Genesis 1 talks about things that are far more spiritually important than whether we and apes descended from common ancestors or how old the universe actually is.

This poem is structured around the number *seven* (the seven days of creation), which is an important key to unlocking the whole thing, as the poem seems to be building up to what happens on the seventh day. But before we go there, let's think about days 1–6. Here's a brief reminder of what is created on those days:

1. Light and dark
2. Waters and sky
3. Land and plant life
4. Sun and moon
5. Fish and birds
6. Animals and humans

When you're reading through those, the problem really doesn't emerge until day four, right? How can light be created on day one while the sun and the stars (the sources of light in the universe) aren't created until several days later?

If this is supposed to be a science textbook, we have a major problem. But if this is a poem, here's a clue that maybe something else is going on. I think it's easiest to make this clear if we put days 1–3 side by side with days 4–6:

1. Light and dark	4. Sun and moon
2. Waters and sky	5. Fish and birds
3. Land and plant life	6. Animals and humans

Are you starting to see it now? One of the layers of truth in this poem is that on the first three days God creates realms, and on the next three days God creates rulers of those realms—the sun and moon to rule over the day and night, and so on.

Then, at the end of the passage about the sixth day things change. The writer starts adding a lot of detail and talks about God creating livestock and wild animals and things that creep upon the ground. Are you still with me? So far, we have a pattern of rulers and realms that has gone as far as the animals. *Then* God creates humanity! What does that say about humanity? That we are the ruler of it all!

But the story doesn't end on the sixth day, does it? Nope, it's all about *seven*, remember? It's the seven days of creation, and the seventh day is nothing like the other six. On the seventh day, God rests. We read that and think nothing of it, but in the ancient world, very few people had the freedom to take time off from work. The only people with significant leisure time were the kings and governors.

What does that say about God? How does that fit into our whole ruler-realm idea? It tells us *God* is the ultimate ruler over it all. That's important because it means that even though humanity has been given the task of caring for creation, we aren't supposed to use it any old way we want. Rather, we are to do what *God* wants for creation. We are to carry out God's will for the earth, because God is its ultimate ruler.

And that's just *one* deep truth contained in the brilliant beginning that opens up the book of Genesis. Now, back to your question: Did Genesis really happen?

Though you can look at Genesis through this sort of science-textbook perspective, there is so much more there than that. If all you look for is science in Genesis, you miss the deeper truths about God, creation, and our purpose in life.

Because the Bible is a religious text, it seems reasonable to think that the most important messages it has are spiritual rather than scientific, and that those are where we should focus our time and energy. When we do that, the conflicts with science fade into the background and we begin to hear the call of God to care for the earth and each other as mutual creations of a loving God. We hear Genesis calling us down the road less traveled and watch as it guides us on a path that leads eventually to Jesus.

Good answers spark new questions:

- What other layers of truth can you see when reading this incredible poem in Genesis 1?
- What might be the reason this passage doesn't sounding like poetry, with a rhyme or a regular meter?

23

How can I hold up my faith against science?

I was sitting at lunch with my new classmates on the first day of school when one of them asked me, "How far is it to the moon?" I was the resident space expert in my group of friends, mostly because I was constantly checking out books about space travel and NASA from the library. But for some reason I had never looked up this question.

That never stopped me from answering, because no one ever knew if I was wrong. "About a thousand miles," I said, with way more confidence than I should have had.

"Actually," came a voice from the end of the table. It was the new kid, Brian. "The moon is actually 238,900 miles from the earth."

Everyone was shocked. Some of my friends started yelling some version of "Oooooo!" or "Daaaaaang!"

Even though we had a rocky start, Brian and I became fast friends, and it didn't take us long to form a space club, where we spent our time quizzing each other about space facts, drawing up prototypes for rockets, and dreaming about being astronauts.

I wonder sometimes about why I made up an answer when I didn't know what I was talking about. I think that same impulse is the source of most of the conflicts I have seen between people's faith and science. Unfortunately, when we make up answers over and over, we can begin to feel like our faith is somehow at war with science.

Before I explain the mistake, let me say this clearly: faith and science are not at war. As you can see in several of the other science chapters in this book, it is entirely possible for you to both believe in the God of the Bible and accept modern science's explanation of the universe and humanity.

But what's the mistake we make? It's a simple one, really, and it's known as "The God of the Gaps." We don't like the unknown. In fact, our brain is wired to fill in gaps. For example, when you see a ball roll behind a wall and come out on the other side, your brain fills in the gap in your understanding by making you believe that it is the same ball that went behind the wall on one side that came out on the other.

That trait in our brain is incredibly helpful ninety-nine percent of the time, but it can go haywire when it comes to bigger things, like science and God. Sometimes when we don't understand something scientifically, our brain reaches out to our faith and fills in the scientific gaps with God.

Let me explain. Before we knew that the earth orbited the sun, people filled in that gap with a God explanation. They reasoned that since God created the earth and made humankind the pinnacle of all creation, the earth must be the center of the universe. Then Galileo offered evidence that the earth was not the center of the universe, and the religious people had major faith issues. They actually argued against the scientific data that the sun is the center of the universe! Why? Because they had filled in a scientific gap with God, and when science filled in the gap with something else, it felt like science was making God smaller or making the Bible less true. But science was doing nothing of the sort! The religious leaders should never have tried to make up an answer to fill in the gaps of science.

The big argument today is not whether or not the earth orbits the sun. Instead, it's about the origins of the universe. Before there were good scientific explanations of how the universe came to be, many people of faith filled in the gap in their scientific knowledge with God explanations. Then we learned a bit about the beginning of the universe. We discovered that as you trace what we know way back to the beginning, we see that a rapid expansion (the Big Bang) fueled the beginning of everything.

When people who had filled in the scientific gaps with God heard that, they had issues, but many of them took comfort in the fact that there was still a little bit of gap left: What made the Big Bang go . . . *bang?* Now a couple solid scientific explanations have come to light to explain what caused the rapid expansion to begin, and people who had filled in that gap are having faith issues again.

The problem with putting God into the gaps of our scientific understanding is that as our scientific understanding expands, it seems to "disprove" the Bible or challenge the power and existence of God.

But the problem in this case is not that science is working against God and the church, but that people do irresponsible things with their theology. Rather than making up answers about God to fill holes in our scientific understanding, we need to construct beliefs about God based on the Bible, not on some area that science hasn't yet been able to explain. When we do that, no amount of scientific discovery can disprove God, because our belief in God doesn't depend on gaps in our scientific understanding.

Let's continue with the origins of the universe. The faith belief here is that God is creator. That is a belief that can be held firmly whether or not you have a scientific understanding of how God created everything. And if you don't run ahead of the belief and start creating a bunch of smaller beliefs, such as "God created everything using divine vocal chords to speak Hebrew words," you're good. As long as you stay with the deep biblical truth (God is creator), the science is just a further extension of that truth. The more you learn about how the universe came to be, the more you discover about how *God* created it!

So, when you're tempted to fill in part of your understanding about the world with something about God, stop. Take a breath and resist the temptation. Instead of just filling all the holes in your mind with God, think, research, and discover the answer. If you can make this your habit, you'll save yourself a lot of frustration as you learn more and more about the amazing world God created!

Good answers spark new questions:

- What is a belief about God that doesn't require a gap in scientific understanding?

- Thinking about God and science this way, could science ever disprove God's existence?

- Are there ways we make the same "God of the gaps" mistake in other fields of study?

24

What's the deal with dinosaurs?

We had just left Disney World, and I was excited because for the first time, I got to ride in the front seat of the minivan on a big trip. It was late and dark as we drove back to my grandparents' house several hours away. I was surprised by how much brighter all the headlights seemed from the front seat. Sometimes I found myself squinting as the big trucks passed us, wondering how my dad could see anything as they drove by.

But I had a question for my dad. A big one. I had been saving it up for this moment because I knew I would have him all to myself as my mom and brother slept in the back. I couldn't wait to hear his answer. As far as I was concerned, he was the smartest person I had ever known. It seemed like anytime I asked him anything, he had an answer.

I had seen the movie *Back to the Future* in which one of the characters was warned by a scientist that if they messed things up when they traveled back into the past, they would create another possible future and might not be able to get back to their current time. I had spent an enormous amount of time thinking about this and had figured out that if that were possible, it might mean that every decision we made created a different universe.

As we drove down the highway, I asked my dad just that. Is that what happened? If so, how did you know if you were creating a different universe? Also, did the other universes keep going, or did they stop happening when you made a choice?

After my long list of deep questions, my dad said nothing. For a second, I wondered if he was asleep at the wheel or if he just wasn't listening. I studied his face and could see he was thinking, so I decided to wait. I hated it when people interrupted *my* deep thoughts.

He did speak eventually, but what he said surprised me: "I don't know." I felt like I had never heard those words come out of his mouth before.

"But . . . I mean, what do you *think?*"

"I think we don't know, and we can't know at this point."

I was stunned. I thought Dad would have a lot to say about my questions. But he explained that there wasn't any data on time travel or on the nature of how time may or may not divide. Even worse, there wasn't really a clear way we could even try to come up with an answer based on scientific data. Anything we could come up with would just be an educated guess.

I think about that conversation with my dad every time someone asks me about dinosaurs and the Bible, because it's the basic answer to the Bible-osaurus question: we don't know, and we can't know. By that I mean that the Bible doesn't say anything at all about dinosaurs.

Don't get me wrong—I've heard a million theories about dinosaurs in the Bible. I've heard everything from dinosaurs being the devil or other angels kicked out of heaven, to them being the Nephilim (Genesis 6:4) just before the story of Noah, to them not even being real at all but, rather, that "dinosaur bones" were something God put in the ground to test our faith.

The problem with all these theories is that they put things into the Bible that aren't there. Either they misinterpret words to mean more than they do (like with the Nephilim), completely make up things that aren't there at all (the devil and fallen angels), or totally contradict science (bones hidden by God).

This question does bring up an idea that is important to know: the Bible doesn't address every issue specifically, and that's okay. However, I don't think there is any part of our lives that the Bible doesn't address. Let's think about those two ideas.

First, the Bible doesn't give specific insight into every issue. Depending on what part of the Bible you are reading, it was written somewhere between 2,000 and 6,000 years ago. That means that most ideas, discoveries, and pieces of information that have been thought of or invented since then won't be discussed specifically. If you want to know whether or not God thinks iPhones or Androids are better, you're going to have to keep wondering, because it won't be in the Bible. Basically, all of modern science fits into this category. Our modern scientific concepts, discoveries, and ways of thinking about life simply weren't around when the Bible was written. Therefore, anything you find in the Bible that you think addresses some modern scientific concept or discovery will have to be, at most, just a hint in that direction.

That's not to dismiss the Bible and say it has nothing to contribute about the modern world. Even though it was written a long time ago to people in a very different culture and world, the stories, poetry, and laws it contains can reach beyond their moment in history, as long as we are careful with them.

That's the incredible thing about the Bible. Even though it was written to people living before, say, the invention of gunpowder, it is the Word of God, and as we read it, we hear the voice of God speaking across the millennia to us today. But because we are so far removed from the time in which it was written, we have to be careful to not make it address the modern day too specifically.

For example, if we read a Bible verse forbidding people from having statues in their house, we need to stop before we dump all our knickknacks and sculptures into the trash. We need to understand what was happening to the people originally addressed by those words. Why did they have statues? What was it about the statues that made God tell them to throw the statues away?

In the case of statues, it was usually because in those days, most religions used statues as idols to represent other gods. Once we understand that, we can take the bigger idea into our modern time and try to apply it. If the statue thing was about not worshipping other gods, what is it in our world that might tempt us to do the same thing? When we find the answer to that question, we can act accordingly and remove from our lives and homes whatever tempts us to worship other gods.

But what about the dinosaurs? Since the Bible doesn't say anything about the dinosaurs specifically, we have bigger things that we can say about them. When I think about the dinosaurs, the words that come to my mind are from Habakkuk 3:2a: "LORD, I have heard of your fame; I stand in awe of your deeds, LORD. . . ."

When I think about the dinosaurs, about their beauty, size, and incredible variety, I am amazed by them. I am in awe. Those of us whose imaginations are captured by the incredible animals that dinosaurs were can allow that wonder to stretch beyond the dinosaurs themselves to God. Or, to paraphrase Psalm 19:1, "The [dinosaurs] declare the glory of God."

Good answers spark new questions:
- What is something kind of weird that you remember from the Bible? How can you understand that in a way that says something about today?
- What is it about saying or hearing the answer "I don't know" or "We can't know" that makes some people feel uncomfortable?

Questions about Life

25

How do I know that God hears all my prayers?

My middle school youth leader, Ms. Pat, had a voice that made me feel at home. I don't know if it was because she sounded like my mom or because she had a slow, southern accent like my grandmother, but something about her voice calmed my middle school attention deficit disorder (ADD) to the point that I could listen to her talk forever. I thought she had to be the closest person to God I knew. When she taught us at church on Sunday nights, she always had stories about how God had helped her or spoken to her. Today was no exception.

"Last Tuesday I was praying over all the people on my prayer list, and—"

She was interrupted by Angela. "Did you pray for my aunt? Is she on your list?"

"Yes, she's on my list. I prayed for her."

"Awesome! She got out of the hospital this week!"

"That's great, Angela."

"I know! I'm so glad she's back home!"

"Me too. But let me get back to my story. I was praying over my prayer list and I kept getting distracted."

Wait. Ms. Pat got distracted while she was praying? Wow! I got distracted while I was praying all the time. I thought that meant I wasn't doing it right!

"I just kept thinking about a friend of mine in my Sunday school class. I would read a name and start praying and then forget what I was praying about and start thinking about my friend. It was frustrating. I kept trying and trying to get to the end of my list but just couldn't do it. Then I realized that it was the Lord trying to tell me to call this friend. So I did, and she answered the phone crying."

I asked the obvious question: "What was she crying about?"

"She'd just gotten some really bad news and was feeling really sad. She said she had felt all alone and asked God why he never gave her any friends. When I called, it was like God answering her and saying, 'I did give you friends, silly.' Which is what I told her. She has a lot of friends. She at least has a whole Sunday school class of friends, and that's more than a lot of people I know."

I love being around people like Ms. Pat because when they talk, you feel like they know God personally. I kind of imagine that they sit down for tea with God a couple times a week and just hang out together. It seemed like every time she prayed, she knew God was really listening to her. She was as confident in her conversations with God as she was with anyone she talked to on earth.

When I had this same question—How do we know God hears us?—she was the one I felt I had to ask. I'll never forget her answer. She said that most of the time when she prayed, she'd get a feeling like God had heard her, or she would have a moment like the one with the friend in her Sunday school class where she felt God had spoken back to her. But sometimes, she said, it felt like her prayers bounced off the ceiling. It was like she picked up a phone to talk to God and there was no one on the other end.

I knew exactly what that felt like. That was my experience *most* of the time when I was praying. I said words, but they seemed to be just words I was saying to the air.

Then she said one last thing that helped me more than just about anything else: "But I believe that God even hears those prayers. I just have to get better at hearing God's response. And the only way you get better at hearing God's voice is by spending more time listening to it."

That made so much sense. The reason she was better at hearing God speak and knowing that her prayers had been heard wasn't because she was closer to God than I was or because God loved her more. She was better at it because she had more practice.

I can tell you that is true. After spending many more years praying to God, I am much better at hearing God's voice now than I used to be. I have much more confidence in my prayers, and I have a lot more prayers in general. Part of that is because I now have discovered that prayer is far bigger than I understood when I was in middle school and learning from Ms. Pat.

You can always tell when someone hasn't discovered how big prayer is because they talk about praying to God as if God is a sort of biblical genie in a bottle. They say things like, "I prayed about passing that test, but God didn't answer me." By that they mean they asked God to make them pass the test and they didn't.

It took me a while to break out of that mindset. The first step for me was realizing that when I prayed, sometimes God wouldn't say yes. Sometimes God would say no, and sometimes God would say "Not right now" or "Maybe later." That was a good step because it meant I had realized that God didn't just do whatever I wanted to happen. But the way I was thinking about prayer still made prayer far too small. I still thought prayer was about me asking God to do things.

Prayer is much bigger than that. Prayer is a conversation with God. When we are doing prayer well, it requires the same kind of concentration as when we are hanging out with a friend and talking about what happened over the weekend. There is a back-and-forth to prayer, in which we talk and then listen and then talk and then listen some more. Prayer is not just a way to get someone with magic powers to do something you can't accomplish. It's a way that we grow closer in our relationship with God. The more we spend time in this conversation, the better we get at recognizing God's voice and being open with our own thoughts and hearts.

Though we want to be comfortable talking to God like a friend, the reality is that we are talking to the creator of the universe. On top of that, we might be trying to talk about things like forgiveness or sin or some other massive subject, and those things can be hard to express off the top of our heads. Many people find that using prayers written by other people helps them find the words to express their hearts to God. That's why people have created prayer books for just that purpose. You have an incredible prayer book right in the middle of the Bible: the book of Psalms!

But what about those requests we make of God? How do we know when God has answered them? The beginning of my answer to that is a couple paragraphs back: We have to realize that when we ask God to do something, it's more like asking our parents for something and less like pushing the button on a drink machine. When God answers our requests to do something, sometimes it happens miraculously, sometimes it doesn't happen at all, and sometimes it goes in a different direction than we could have anticipated.

In my life I see that, most often, God's answers to my prayers come through people around me. Let me give you an example. A while ago, I had a major project that was getting close to launching and had me majorly stressed out. I had no idea how it was going to go or what was going to happen after. There was not much more I could do to change the outcome, so I had been asking God to give me peace. It wasn't working. I kept praying for peace, and each day kept bringing more and more stress.

Then my friend Sam came over to hang out, and as we sat in my living room talking about this project and my stress, he told me a story about a friend of ours. It was a simple story about how our friend had needed multiple tries to make something happen. When Sam finished the story, I felt a wave of peace come over me. It was the kind of peace the Bible talks about in Philippians 4:7—a peace that passed all understanding. God had used Sam to bring into my life the peace I had needed all week long.

Let me try to put all of this together. How can you know that God hears your prayers? First, your prayers need to be more than a list of things you want God to miraculously do in your life. Prayer should be a way for you to spend time with God. There is a back-and-forth to a good prayer life that *sometimes*, but not always, includes things you need God to do. Knowing that God hears you in those times grows out of spending time with God in prayer. The more you pray, the better you get at sensing God's presence and understanding God's voice. When it comes to asking God to do things, sometimes they happen like you want, sometimes not, and a lot of times, God sends people to be there with you and help you with whatever you've been asking God to do.

Here's the coolest part about that last sentence: if God uses people to answer prayers, that means *you* can be used by God as the answer to someone else's prayer! As we listen to people in our world who need help, as we hear people asking for prayer about struggles in their lives, we can try to be God's answer to those prayers. We can comfort those who are having a hard time. We can be a friend to those who are lonely, and we can give advice to those who aren't sure which way to go. I pray that God will show you how to be the answer to someone else's prayers this week!

Good answers spark new questions:

- Why might God tell you no when you're asking for something that would be good?

- Why do you think some people only want to use prayers that they come up with on the spot instead of also using prayers written by other people and published in prayer books?

26

What about people who claim to be Christians and then do terrible things?

One day I had to stay late at school for practice, and when I got home, my parents were already watching the nightly news. It was bad. A group of people who called themselves Christians had bombed an abortion clinic. People were dead.

I wondered how any Christian could think that was an okay thing to do. Then the people who were part of the group that had planted the bomb started talking about how this was a battle in a war. They used all kinds of violent language like that to explain their actions. I didn't know what to think, and I was so upset that I could only eat one plate of food for dinner. (I was usually hungry enough for seconds.)

The next day at school was hard. I had made friends with a bunch of people who were not Christians. They were always saying things to me like, "I don't really like Christians, but you're not like that. You're nicer." I knew they would have a lot to say about this. They did. All day long I heard kids talk about how evil the people who had bombed the abortion clinic were, and I agreed. They had done something terrible. But then my friends would start in on Christianity and how it had enabled these people to do this awful thing. I tried my best to stick up for my faith, but it was hard after what people claiming to be Christians had done. The next day was not as difficult, and a couple weeks later things were almost back to normal.

Unfortunately, this happens over and over. People do horrible things—and sometimes those people are Christians. Throughout history people have found ways to use the Bible to support everything from the Crusades to American slavery to the Holocaust. Though they can find parts of the Bible that seem to support what they say and do, they are usually doing something very dangerous with the Bible. But the crazy thing is, it's something we all have a tendency to do. It's called prooftexting.

Prooftexting is when you take a verse or a section of the Bible out of its context and use it as proof for your argument. For example, when you're arguing with your parents, you might say that Jesus said in Luke 14:26, "If anyone comes to me and does not hate father and mother, . . . such a person cannot be my disciple." "So," you would rationalize, "I hate you in the name of Jesus!" That's a little ridiculous. No responsible pastor or Bible scholar will tell you that Jesus is instructing children to actually hate their parents. Jesus is using dramatic phrasing to emphasize how much you should love him. He is saying that you should love Jesus so much that the love for your father and mother pales—looks like hate—in comparison.

But if you think about everything that happens in the Bible, you can quickly see how people can pull out tiny parts and link them together in a way that can justify doing almost anything. That's why it's so important to be careful about how we read and use the Bible.

I find that even when we don't want to, we can start prooftexting without even realizing it. As we read the Bible, it's easy to ignore the parts that disagree with our beliefs and pay attention only to the parts that match our perspective. Most of the time we don't even notice we're doing it. But there's a simple test to figure out if you've fallen into prooftexting.

If you find that the Bible always agrees with you, most likely you're doing some amount of prooftexting as you read it.

When we read the Bible, we need to let it reveal our own faults and challenge us to live differently. As we dive into the stories of Scripture, we must be careful not only to identify with the good characters, but to find what we have in common with the bad ones so we can see what parts of our lives need repentance, forgiveness, and change.

But what about those people who do truly horrible things? Are they Christians? Will they go to heaven?

When you look at all of the Bible, you see a loving God who does extravagant things to forgive and fix all the brokenness caused by sin. That God calls people not just to be recipients of divine grace, but to be the agents of it in the world. God calls us to be a living presence of God's love and forgiveness in the world. You can't escape that, and wherever you find people calling themselves Christians while spewing hatred, vengeance, and unforgiveness, you have found people who are neither following the Bible nor communicating its message in their speech and actions. They might call themselves Christians, but they are not reflecting the heart and soul of Christianity in what they do.

So, what about heaven? Will Christians who do terrible things go to heaven? That's harder to answer because 99 percent of the time, we find God's love and forgiveness comforting, but when we come up against what we experience as evil, it can be hard to take. Yet, even though we may say that someone's actions don't reflect the Christian faith, God is incredibly loving and forgiving. God can forgive absolutely anything—even the most horrible atrocities. Yes, God can forgive evil people. The Bible is full of murderers and adulterers and all kinds of bad people whom God not only forgave but used to do wonderful, loving, grace-filled things.

What that means is that *we* don't get to decide whether or not those people will be in heaven. *We* don't decide their eternal destiny; God does. All we can do is pray that God will change them, do our best to steer clear of the patterns of thought and behavior that allow people to do such horrible things, and do our best to be a brighter beacon of love than they are of hatred.

That's where the power is. Those friends of mine who were so mad about the news focused their anger on Christianity, but after the news faded, I was still there. Every day when I sat down in class or hung out with them after school, I had the opportunity to show them that Christians are loving and forgiving. Though the horrible people had a big splash in the news that day, I had hundreds more days to shine the true light of Jesus in my world. And many of those people who began by attacking Christianity ended up deciding that the love and forgiveness I offered was the true Christianity. Some of them even chose to follow Jesus as a result. That's the real power: the power of Jesus' love to change people's hearts.

Whenever you see people calling themselves Christians and doing awful things, know that in your part of the world, you have far more power than they do to impact people because you are there every day. I pray that you will take that seriously and use this day to love someone like Jesus loves them.

Good answers spark new questions:

- Could God have forgiven Judas, the disciple who betrayed Jesus? What about Hitler?

- Why do you think God doesn't allow us to decide who is going to heaven?

27

Is it harder to be a Christian if I have ADD?

I was searching my backpack for the third time in a row before math started. We had to turn in a major homework assignment that I had finished the night before, and I couldn't find it anywhere. What was even crazier was that my mom had reminded me to take it right before we left, and I remembered putting it in my backpack and walking out the door.

But no matter how much I searched, it just wasn't there, so I walked up to the teacher for what seemed like the millionth time to tell her that I couldn't find my homework. "Ms. Smith, I finished my packet last night and my mom reminded me to put it in my backpack this morning, but I can't find it."

"Really?" I could tell she thought I was lying. I couldn't blame her. I would probably think I was lying too.

"Yes. I swear I did it. I just can't find it."

"Well, if you don't find it before the end of class, you'll get a zero for an entire week's homework."

"I know. Is there anything I can do? Can you give me another packet or something?"

"Jeremy, I'm sorry. You're going to have to learn a lesson this time. I can't keep making exceptions for you."

I didn't respond. I just walked away. It wasn't that I hadn't done the work; it had just gotten lost between my house and my classroom. It happened to me lot. And homework was just the tip of the iceberg. There was also the way my mind often felt like it switched channels uncontrollably in the middle of class and started thinking about something else, and the number of times I started something only to leave it a couple minutes later and start something else (and never finish either thing).

Anyone who knew the signs of attention deficit disorder, or ADD, could have diagnosed me, but at that time no one did. Not until I was in my twenties did a counselor tell me I had one of the worst cases of ADD she had ever seen.

She put me on medicine, and I couldn't believe it! I had so much more control and was able to stay on task almost without even trying! I had no idea how much my ADD had shaped my life in negative ways, but I soon found there were upsides to it as well. My distractible brain was really helpful when trying to be funny, and it was incredible at helping me discover fresh perspectives that no one else in the room had considered.

For whatever reason, people can be super-negative about ADD to the point that it can be intensely embarrassing for people to admit that they have it and/or that they take medicine to help them overcome the bad sides to it. If you know people who have ADD, be careful how you talk about it around them. They are likely sensitive about it and don't want to be treated like they are somehow immature or irresponsible because they have it. Oh yeah, and they definitely don't want you to ask them if they've taken their medicine.

If you are a person with ADD, you need to know that you don't need to be ashamed about it. People's brains are wired in all kinds of different ways, and some people have brains that end up making them have ADD. The way we often teach doesn't always work best for people like me who have ADD. That's why we have medicine and coping techniques to help us pay attention and stop the channels from changing in our brain when we need to be fully present.

Some scientists think that ADD developed to help ancient hunters be better at finding and killing animals for food. If instead of sitting at a desk in a classroom, you were holding a spear in the middle of the woods, having ADD could be really helpful. In that situation, you don't want to be super-focused on one thing. You need your attention to shift when you hear a stick crack under the paw of an animal behind you.

But what about Christianity? Is it harder to be a Christian if you have ADD? Harder to study the Bible? Harder to pray? Harder to listen for God's leading in your life?

Maybe some things are harder with ADD—but having ADD will *never* make you a worse Christian than someone without the disorder. In fact, I'm convinced that some of the main characters in the Bible had ADD. Peter is a perfect example. Several stories featuring Peter remind me of the symptoms of ADD. Remember the story when he sees Jesus walking on the water, and without even thinking, he asks if he can try to do it too—and then was quickly distracted by the waves? There are also a lot of instances when Peter says things without thinking, like when he suggests they build houses for Jesus, Moses, and Elijah at Jesus' transfiguration. That was kind of a random thing to say, Peter!

But there was also the beautiful moment when Jesus asked the disciples about who he was. The others gave stock answers they had heard other places, like that Jesus was Moses or one of the other prophets who had come back to earth. Peter's answer came out of left field. It was a completely new perspective, and a bit dangerous to suggest: Jesus was the Messiah.

I love reading about Peter in the Gospels because I feel like I am that person. I have crazy moments when I say something I shouldn't, but I also have moments when I come up with a new way of thinking about something that really helps people see the Bible from a fresh perspective.

Then there's something called hyperfocus. One of the attributes of ADD that can be really confusing to people who don't have the condition is the ability of a person with ADD to hyperfocus on a single thing for an extended period of time. It doesn't happen all the time, but it's an incredible way in which people with ADD are sometimes able to finish a project. I think this attribute of ADD actually helps in a specific area of faith: prayer. Not just any prayer, but the ancient mystical prayer practices. Many of them require a hyperfocus kind of ability and are tailor-made for people with ADD. If you want to try some of them, just google "centering prayer" or "*lectio divina.*"

Yes, having ADD can *help* you grow as a Christian!

Look, if being a Christian required you to sit still and learn by paying attention to a lecture all the time, I'd say ADD would make it harder. But that's not the core of Christianity. The only reason ADD will hold you back from having a deep relationship with God is if you let our culture's stigma toward ADD shame you into feeling less than others. Otherwise, I think your ADD will be just like any other part of you. In the right circumstances it will help you, and in the wrong ones it will hurt you. But don't worry: if having ADD my whole life has taught me anything, it's that God is used to it and loves my *whole* ADD self.

If you have ADD, here's my advice. Next time someone makes a joke about you not being able to concentrate in Sunday school, remember that I think Peter had ADD, and he was one of the most important leaders in the church. *And* he walked on water! I mean, if you want to be one of the normal disciples back in the boat, that's cool and all, but give me a stroll on the water any day.

Good answers spark new questions:

- In what other ways can ADD help you grow closer to God?

- Are there other psychological conditions that our society treats as completely bad that could actually help someone's faith? What about physical or intellectual disabilities?

28

What does the Bible say about drinking and drugs?

Every Christmas I would stare at the manger scene in the nook that was part of my mom's special cabinet. Unlike the rest of the cabinet, this part didn't have a glass door in front of it. That detail is important. The fact that there was no glass protecting the manger scene seemed to mean that it was okay for me to play with it.

Not only that, but the manger scene looked to me like an awesome setup full of action figures like the ones I played with every day. There was even a row of lights in the top of the cabinet that you could turn on to make it "come to life," like the characters were sitting on a little stage. But this set was, as my mom said, "to look at, not to play with!" And my parents reminded me of this fact every time I started to stare at it.

But there were lights! And action figures dressed in awesome robes! And a baby, and animals! Animals, I tell you! It was as if every time I walked by, the cow was saying, "Moo! Play with me . . . *moooooo!*"

One day it was all too much. My parents were busy hanging out with their friends in the other room, and I decided to go look at the manger scene. As soon as I climbed up on a stool to peer in, the cow started asking me to play, and then the donkey chimed in. Then, as I looked down at baby Jesus, he reached his arms up to me like he was saying, "Hold me."

I mean, who can say no to baby Jesus? So I crept my hand into the manger scene, avoiding the shepherd's staff and being careful not to hit the wise man's crown. And for a second, I did it! I picked up Jesus without destroying the whole manger scene! I was so excited that I jerked my hand out of the scene to play with him, and with my hand came all the other pieces. The wise men flung against the opposite wall, the shepherds toppled onto the floor, and the cow hit me in the face on its way down.

It was the cow that was the problem. I was so surprised when it hit my head that I lost my balance and fell off the stool with baby Jesus in my hand. I did a quick survey of the pieces, and to my surprise, all of them were okay . . . except for the shepherd, whose staff had broken under my hand when I fell. I was extra careful as I picked up each piece and set it back in its place. I laid the shepherd's broken staff in front of him, hoping my mom wouldn't notice—but knowing, with a sinking feeling, that she probably would and, before too long, would want to have a talk about what had happened to her precious manger scene.

I think about this incident whenever someone asks me about drinking and drugs. Playing with my mom's manger scene seemed enticing and harmless—and drinking and drugs can often seem that way too, in the moment. But then, if you're not careful, you can break things and cause a lot of problems.

What does the Bible say about drinking and drugs? I think you might be surprised.

When we talk about drugs, we have a bit of a problem because the Bible doesn't mention them *specifically*. There is no commandment that says, "Thou shalt not smoke marijuana." But the Bible has plenty of things to say that address the issue of drug use. You just have to think a little harder.

With just a bit of extra thought, we can discover a bigger theme that deals with how we use our bodies. For instance, 1 Corinthians 6:19-20 says, "Do you not know that your bodies are temples of the Holy Spirit, who is in you, whom you have received from God? You are not your own; you were bought at a price. Therefore honor God with your bodies." Passages like this reveal a bigger theme: take care of your body. There are many, many Bible verses dedicated to helping people take good care of their bodies. Some of them prescribe how to deal with illness, and others talk about how to prepare food so that people don't get sick.

Why is the Bible so concerned with our bodies? It's simple: the healthier we are, the more time and energy we will have to help others and do what God needs us to do to make earth look more like heaven. When it comes to drugs, the answer is easy: they damage our bodies. Period. Though they may flood our brains with chemicals that make us feel good in the moment, they ultimately damage our bodies and can severely damage the development of your brain. So, when it comes to drugs, the Bible is clear: don't do them.

Drinking is different though, right? Some amount of different types of alcohol can be good for you, especially as you get older. There are studies, for instance, that indicate that small amounts of red wine are good for your heart, and you may have noticed your parents or other adults drinking a little bit of alcohol from time to time. Not only that, but the Bible even sometimes talks about drinking in a positive way. For example, Paul writes to a younger church leader, Timothy, "Stop drinking only water, and use a little wine because of your stomach and your frequent illnesses" (1 Timothy 5:23).

On top of that, the Bible is full of references to basically every important person drinking wine. At the Last Supper, when Jesus began the Sacrament of Holy Communion, even he was drinking wine and offering it to the disciples.

Why, then, do some Christians say you shouldn't drink wine? There are really three main arguments people make: The first is that though the Bible has a lot of positive things to say about wine and shows it included in many holy ceremonies, the Bible never has good things to say about being drunk. Whenever you see a version of the word *drunk* in the Bible, it is talking about something negative. Because of these passages, many people say that they don't want to drink because they don't want to be tempted to drink too much and become drunk. Being drunk is not just bad for your body; it can also lead to other problems that hurt you and the people around you, like alcoholism, irresponsible behavior, and drunk driving.

The second perspective on drinking comes from a passage in the Bible talking about helping each other out. Romans 14:13 says, "Therefore let us stop passing judgment on one another. Instead, make up your mind not to put any stumbling block or obstacle in the way of a brother or sister." The passage goes on to talk about avoiding eating or drinking things that other people think are sinful. Some people use this passage to say that because some people are tempted to drink too much, we should avoid it altogether to not cause someone else to stumble.

Finally, the Bible has things to say about breaking the law. Assuming the laws are not asking you to sin, Romans 13:1 says, "Let everyone be subject to the governing authorities, for there is no authority except that which God has established. The authorities that exist have been established by God." That means that God wants us to obey the law. And right now, in just about every country, it is against the law for kids to drink alcohol. As a society, we've decided that it's best to wait with drinking until you've gained some life experience and maturity so that if you do decide to drink, you can do so responsibly and in moderation.

Drinking and doing drugs may look like harmless fun in the moment, like the cow that was calling out to me in the manger scene. People in your life might be calling out to you right now, encouraging you to break the rules and try drugs or alcohol. I know that those temptations and pressures are hard to resist. But the rules are there for your protection.

God wants you to be healthy and able to live a full, joyful life. To help you do that, God has given you the gift of guiding principles in the Bible backed up by the laws and rules of our society and households.

Good answers spark new questions:

- Are there other things people avoid doing because they cause others to stumble?

- What do you think the Bible would want you to do if a law was unjust?

29

Are we supposed to think about God every second of the day? How are we supposed to live like Jesus every day?

As we left Sunday school one day, my teacher handed each of us a card with a Bible verse on it. She said that these verses were some of the shortest in the Bible, and she wanted us each to memorize our verse before class next week. Then she sweetened the deal: if we had memorized our verse when we came to class next week, she would give us one of those suckers with bubble gum in the middle. I loved those things!

As I left the class, I was excited to see that my verse had only two words: "Pray continually." It was from 1 Thessalonians 5:17. I could practically taste the sucker already! I would get watermelon!

On my way home, I started thinking about the verse more than the candy and wondered how praying continually was even possible. How could someone pray *all the time*? I didn't think I could do *anything* all the time. I mean, you have to sleep some of the time, right? I figured the verse didn't mean I had to pray while I was sleeping, but that didn't really make it a lot easier.

I thought maybe the card was wrong or was missing something, so when we got home, I got my Bible out and turned to the Contents page to figure out where 1 Thessalonians was, then flipped to chapter 5. Looking up the passage didn't help. I discovered that my memory verse was part of a longer passage that said, "Rejoice always, pray continually, give thanks in all circumstances; for this is God's will for you in Christ Jesus" (vv. 16–18).

Okay, how was I supposed to simultaneously rejoice, pray, *and* give thanks? I was having a hard enough time figuring out how to do just one of those things all the time, and now I was supposed to do *all* of them! How could you ever pay attention to someone else or do math problems or listen to music if you were busy doing all those things? I had no idea how to answer these questions, so I decided to ask my Sunday school teacher next week.

The time came, and I said my verse to get my candy. Then I asked my teacher, "How can you pray continually? Also, the verse before it says 'Rejoice always,' and the verse after says to always give thanks. I don't get it."

She explained that these verses were not about literally doing these things all the time. They were saying we should live our lives with the same attitude that we have when we're rejoicing or praying or giving thanks. That made a lot more sense.

The Bible is full of statements like these that talk about something in the most extreme way to emphasize it. The word for that is *hyperbole*. Pastors do the same thing when they tell us to think about God all the time or make sure we are living like Jesus every day. It doesn't mean we should never think about anything *but* Jesus or that we need to turn into some sort of God robot and only do things we think Jesus actually did.

The idea is to try really hard to make everything we do and say and think be godly. When I put it that way, it sounds obvious, right? Why even bother saying it? *Of course* we should try to follow Jesus all the

Are we supposed to think about God every second of the day?
How are we supposed to live like Jesus every day?

time! But even though it may sound obvious, it's still worth saying and thinking about. You see, far too often we tend to divide our lives into different parts. We have the school part, the church part, the home part, the sports part, and on and on. If we aren't careful, we can start acting one way in the school part and a different way in the church part. Sometimes we passionately sing praise to God at church and then go to school and bully someone until they cry. That's not okay. Instead, we want to try to let our faith influence all the parts of our life so that, hopefully, all of our actions in all the parts of our lives are done in a way that honors God.

When we do that, it's like we are "thinking about God" all the time. We are "living like Jesus every day." And in a way, we are even "praying continually." So, don't get caught up on those extreme words when you read them in the Bible or hear your pastor say them. Take a moment to think about what simpler thing they might be pointing to, and try for that!

Good answers spark new questions:
- What other extreme statements have you heard pastors or other Christian leaders make that seem impossible? What were they really trying to say?

Are we supposed to think about God every second of the day?
How are we supposed to live like Jesus every day?

149

Group Guide

The questions in this book are explored best in community. Over and over again in the New Testament Jesus both models community and implores us to engage in community. For each chapter, I have pulled out a related scripture, explained how it relates to the chapter, and offered a couple of discussion ideas and questions to hopefully give you enough of a start to use this book as the content for your small group or Sunday School class.

Chapter: Is it okay to have questions and doubts about Christianity?

Scripture: John 20:19-29

Explanation: This is the scripture referenced in this chapter, but it is full of all kinds of beautiful detail for people who have questions about their faith. Take a moment to note the similarities between when Jesus appears to his disciples in the beginning of the selection and when he appears again the second time. The two appearances are almost identical in the beginning. This serves to underscore the fact that Jesus came back for Thomas. Also significant is the role of Thomas's friends in this situation where they allow him space, but don't forget him. In fact, it seems like they cannot wait to go tell him in hopes that he would return.

Explore: Have students identify the common traits of the two appearances. What is different? Where do they see themselves in the story are they more Thomas or more one of the other disciples? How can they live out this story in their lives?

Chapter: How do we know God exists?

Scripture: Luke 24:13-35

Explanation: This chapter talks about the fact that our own encounters with God are a powerful proof of the existence of God. A lot of times those experiences aren't like Moses and the burning bush. Rather, the

Emmaus experience in this passage is one that parallels many people's experience of God. Sometimes we encounter God before we even realize it. Then, once we understand God a little better, we see that we had been having those encounters all along our way.

Explore: Talk to your students about what it is like to encounter God. Offer your own story and ask for theirs. Ask them what they think it means when the people said "Were not our hearts burning within us while he talked with us on the road and opened the Scriptures to us?"

Chapter: Who created God?

Scripture: Jeremiah 1:5 (and any other verses that use "before" and "after")

Explanation: In this chapter we explore the idea that if God created time, then God exists outside of time. That means that time words don't describe God accurately. The time words we use to describe God are really the best we can do as time-bound beings to describe what it's like to interact with a being that exists outside of time. And, that is how we make sense of verses like this one that sound so weird. God knew us before we were born? That only makes sense when we understand God's relation time as something different than out relation to time.

Explore: Use this and other scriptures to talk about how we, who only know what it's like to live bound to time, describe our interactions with a time-less being. It will be very abstract and a lot of fun for your students who like to experiment with interesting and challenging ideas.

Chapter: Are we supposed to love God, or Jesus, or both?

Scripture: Ecclesiastes 4:9-12

Explanation: This is one of the classic verses that talks about the power of relationships. Though this verse talks about it in a very utilitarian way, so you will want to try to push beyond the usefulness of relationship to really engage in the more mystical sense of relationship.

Explore: One of the most accessible ways to explore the idea of the Trinity is to explore the relationships in the lives of the students. How do those relationships bind them together? How does being a friend with someone change them? What about family? This verse talks about working together and ends with the image of being "braided" together. How does that explain our lives and help us understand the Trinity?

Chapter: One of my family members who didn't believe in God died. Where are they now?

Scripture: John 14:1-4

Explanation: In the chapter we talked about how the Bible uses figurative language like simile and metaphor to communicate the profound reality of Heaven. One little piece of background to this verse is that the Jewish people throughout their ancient history lived in multi-family homes with many rooms that they would add on to as more people joined the family. In a sense, Jesus is inviting the disciples to become part of his family. You might also google verses about heaven and explore them all as a group with these questions.

Explore: Look at this verse, and imagine what it might be saying about God. What does the metaphor point to? How does that impact our understanding of what happens after we die? How does that understanding impact how we live our lives in the present? How does that express the love, grace, and mercy of God? In this verse specifically, what might it mean to become part of God's family here on earth? What might that require of you?

Chapter: What happens to the people who didn't have the opportunity to learn about Jesus? Do they go to hell when they die?

Scripture: Numbers 22-24 (You select your favorite parts)

Explanation: What Does a talking donkey have to do with people who haven't heard about Jesus? I got you on this one. Balaam is not Jewish. He is a random "seer" (think prophet) who is really good, really well known, and available to help out for the right price. He has not heard about Abraham, has not been part of God's covenant with the people at Sinai, but God still speaks to him. It even says in 24:2 that "the Spirit of God came on him." Wow! The point is that God doesn't have some sort of set of rules as to who God talks to and who gets the silent treatment. God will speak to whoever God wants.

Explore: If God speaks to a non-Jewish prophet, what does that say about our current question? This story has fun playing with words when Balaam is called a famous "seer" but the only one who sees the angel for a while is a donkey. What does that say about Balaam's ability when it comes to God? (Help your students see that Balaam only can see what God has revealed to him.)

Chapter: With all our sins, how can we be sure that we will get to heaven?

Scripture: Matthew 4:18-22

Explanation: This chapter refocuses our mind from obsessing over whether or not we get into heaven or go to hell to focusing on following Jesus. This scripture is the beginning of repeated calls of Jesus to "follow me." This time the call comes to the everyday people who would become Jesus' disciples. It is important to note that rather than asking disciples to apply to follow Jesus as a rabbi (which was the norm at the time), he goes to them. Jesus meets them where they are and calls them to follow him right there.

Explore: All of this is important when we think about what the Christian life and the call of Jesus is in our world. Why do you think Jesus chose to say "follow me" instead of something about "going to heaven?" What is the significance of Jesus going to the disciples in their everyday workplace? How is this scripture echoed in our modern day?

Chapter: Why did God put an option of sinning in our lives? Why didn't God make us so we wouldn't fall into temptation?

Scripture: 1 John 1:8-9

Explanation: Forgiveness is a central concept in Christianity, and this question offers a great opportunity to talk about the power of the forgiveness of God to transform our lives. When you see forgiveness discussed in the New Testament you frequently find it within or next to a discussion on the need for confession. Indeed, how can you ask for forgiveness without recognizing the fact that there is something wrong that needs to be forgiven?

Explore: When have students felt the need for forgiveness from a person in their life? What was that experience like? How did they confess? How was their confession received? How was forgiveness offered or not? How does that experience help them understand God's offer to forgive us?

Chapter: Does God really only give us as much as we can handle?

Scripture: Gal 6:2

Explanation: In the chapter we end up talking about how we can be the way out of difficult situations for our friends. This theme of helping other people (especially our friends and fellow Christians) is repeated over and over in the Bible. This verse makes that concept visual where it talks about bearing each other's burden. The idea of helping someone carry a heavy load is a powerful metaphor. Who hasn't helped someone else carry a couch or something else? When we team up, tasks that are too much become possible.

Explore: Ask students to think about a time when they were in a difficult situation and someone helped them "bear their burden." What about when we see someone we don't know (or don't know well) in a difficult situation? What is our responsibility there?

Chapter: Why do people die in accidents when they are really young?

Scripture: Psalm 22

Explanation: Far too often we think of negative emotions as being somehow less holy or something that we need to get over or hide from God (or at least from our pastor). That is not something you can find from an honest study of the Bible. Rather, what we find in the Bible is real freedom to express the fullness of our emotions to God. A quick look at the Psalms reveals that an enormous number of them revolve around complaining to God or even accusing God of not doing what God committed to do. That is the content of this psalm, and its emotional frankness and raw display of displeasure with God is a model for us to see how we can be open and real with whatever we are feeling.

Explore: Ask students to read the Psalm out loud. Saying these things out loud is even more empowering as some of them almost seem wrong to say for those who have felt a pressure to always be happy and flowery with God. Ask students when they have felt things like this in the past? When they were angry or sad, did they feel they had permission to express that to God? Why is it important to be open with God in prayer?

Chapter: Why is the idea of sex so pleasing?

Scripture: Genesis 2:24

Explanation: Most of the time youth are expecting a negative message about sex from the church, and this is an opportunity to surprise them and talk about it in a positive tone. This passage from Genesis (also quoted by Jesus in Mark 10:8) comes from the beautiful and layered story of Adam and Eve. It is right after the creation of Eve from Adam's rib. This brings marriage and sex back to the very beginning, tying them to the core of our identity as humans. It means that our desire for relationship and intimacy is not a sin, it is what God desired and how God created us. That is good! If you want to go a step further, broaden the passage and include the next verse: they were naked and without shame. Talk about how truly intimate relationships help us accept ourselves and let go of our shame.

Explore: Ask students, in light of this passage of scripture the same question: why is the idea of sex so pleasing? Ask them to look at the ideal relationship modeled here. How does that happen? How can two people trust each other that much? How can two people let go of that much fear? Why is it important to have intimate relationships?

Chapter: Did all the stories in the Bible really happen, or were some of them made up to teach people lessons?

Scripture: Psalm 23

Explanation: In order to experience the power of taking a Bible passage on its own terms rather than assuming it has to be taken literally, look at a clearly metaphorical passage like this one. Psalm 23 is one of the great examples of metaphor in all of literature. Take it apart piece by piece, thinking about what the metaphor meant to the original audience and then finding modern correlations to the concepts you uncover in the process.

Explore: This is an example of the piece by piece questioning you can do: Why is God described as a shepherd? What is the modern day equivalent of a shepherd? How does that help us understand God? How does that call us to act differently in the world?

Chapter: What did Jesus look like?

Scripture: Luke 4:1-13 (esp. v.2)

Explanation: The chapter ends by talking about the fact that Jesus lived a fully human life like us, and as part of that he was tempted. This is stated directly in verse two of this passage. Though the specifics of this passage are interesting to be sure, the big message to focus on is that Jesus was tempted. That means two things. First, since Jesus didn't sin, temptation isn't a sin. Second, and for the same reason, Jesus has the power to overcome temptation. Jesus offers us that ability to us (see Hebrews 2:8 for another good verse about that).

Explore: Begin by simply exploring the reality that Jesus was tempted. Why is that surprising for some people? What does that mean about temptation? How does that help students understand temptation in general? Hopefully you can guide this discussion back to the chapter by pointing out that because we share these experiences with Jesus, we can understand him better and it can help us grow closer to Jesus... even if we don't know exactly how he looked.

Chapter: How do we know that the stuff in the Bible came from God and is important?

Scripture: 2 Timothy 3:16-17

Explanation: Anyone who has been around someone who has died or been to a funeral with an open casket can tell you that there is something strange about that experience because though the person's body is there, the person isn't there. The life is gone from them. Ancient people associated that life with breath. They knew that when people were alive they were breathing, and when they were dead they were not. So they tied the idea of our life and soul to the invisible breath that we breathed. This metaphor makes this passage far more powerful because it implies that the Bible comes from the very life of God.

Explore: What does this understanding of breath add to our understanding of the Bible? What does it mean to teach, rebuke, and train in righteousness (take each one on its own)? How is that done practically speaking? How does all of that change how we approach the Bible?

Chapter: Why do Christians still obey some things the Bible says but ignore others?

Scripture: Matthew 19:16-22

Explanation: In this chapter we talk about how every part of the Bible is important, but we must understand it and apply it in our modern setting. On the face of this passage in the Bible, it seems to say that in order to really follow Jesus, you have to sell everything you have. The challenge will be to help students figure out what Jesus is saying and then help them to apply that to the life of a teen in the 21st century. Rather than requiring everyone to sell everything they have, this passage points out the fact that though the man had followed the details of the law, he had not considered its implications. He had grown to love his money so much that he would choose it over following Jesus. Jesus was challenging him to really serve God first, even above his money.

Explore: Ask students to read the passage and give a simple, literal interpretation that may not make sense in their world. What Does Jesus seem to be saying to this man? (He has to sell everything to be faithful). Do you think Jesus thinks the same thing for you today? If not, what is the bigger idea that Jesus is teaching here?

Chapter: Some people say Islam is the same as Christianity—is that true?

Scripture: Genesis 12:3 and Romans 11:17-18

Explanation: God's goal from the beginning of his promise with Abram was to bless the WHOLE world. This passage in Romans uses the metaphor of a branch being grafted into a well-established plant to explain God opening up the blessing to people who were not Jewish. It is clear that God's overarching orientation to people (whether or not they believe in Jesus) is one of openness and love. That is how we should act towards people of other faiths. Rather than fight and argue, we love, respect and offer the grace of God that God is already offering.

Explore: How big is God's promise to Abram? What part of the earth's inhabitants is God targeting by blessing Abram? How are these two scriptures related? If we are to echo God's actions in our lives, how does this tell us to act towards people of other faiths?

Chapter: If Jews are God's chosen people but they don't believe in Jesus, will they still go to heaven?

Scripture: Matthew 7:21-27

Explanation: This scripture makes surprising revelations about heaven. It says that some people who drove out demons and performed miracles in the name of Jesus will not be in heaven. That is beyond surprising! It makes it clear that ultimately humans have no idea who will or will not be in heaven. There will be some people there we wouldn't think would be there and some people we would think would be there that aren't. But what follows this passage is just as important. Once Jesus removes our delusion that we can know perfectly who goes to heaven and who doesn't, he finishes his sermon talking about following his teaching. In a sense it's like Jesus is saying, "don't spend all your time worrying who will and won't get to heaven. Instead, use that time to focus on following me."

Explore: What is surprising about Jesus' statements about he people who say "Lord, Lord?" What is the basic premise of the parable Jesus tells after that? How might these two passages relate to each other? What might Jesus be saying by putting these two ideas next to each other?

Chapter: How should I talk to atheists and people who don't believe in God?

Scripture: 1 Peter 3:15-16

Explanation: This passage doesn't require a lot of background. It is simple and can be taken quite literally. But what it does say is important. We need to be prepared. How often are Christians presented with the opportunity to share something about their faith, but don't know what to say? That is why we must take these words to heart and know how we can share our faith with gentleness and respect.

Explore: When have you seen someone share their faith with gentleness and respect? When have you seen someone share their faith in a way that was not gentle or respectful? What is something you have learned about God that you would want other people to know? How can you share it with gentleness and respect? Consider pairing students up to practice how they would speak about their faith with gentleness and respect.

Chapter: Should I be friends with people from other religions?

Scripture: 2 Corinthians 2:14

Explanation: This chapter ended by talking about being careful about who your friends are and how they might lead you in a different direction than you are wanting to go. This passage from 2 Corinthians is written to a people who were in a city filled with people who worshipped other gods and did so in very taboo ways. There was a very real temptation for them to leave the worship of Jesus and start worshipping other gods. However, it is the "yoke" metaphor that is most powerful for this discussion. If you imagine people who are going in different directions being tied to each other like two oxen being tied together to pull a plow, what happens? Their directions are altered. They no longer will be moving in the direction they originally intended. This is a powerful image for friendship. The closer you are to a friend the more you are "yoked" to them and the more their desires and life choices will influence your own. So, be careful about who you "yoke" yourself to.

Explore: Talk through the yoke metaphor with your students. Ask them to share times when friends have influenced their decisions in good and bad ways. Then ask them to share the same about when they influenced their friends decisions. Then, invite students to think about where they want to be headed and compare that to where their closest friends are headed. Are they "yoked" to the right people?

Chapter: Did God create other universes?

Scripture: Psalm 19:1-6

Explanation: The biggest idea in this chapter is that if there are other universes, God created them too. This poem from the book of Psalms echoes another big idea from the Bible: God is revealed through everything God creates. That makes the idea of other universes even more interesting.

Explore: When are some times that you experienced God through creation? If God is revealed through God's creation and if God created multiple universes, what would that reveal about God?

Chapter: Why do scientists believe that God didn't create the Earth?

Scripture: Joshua 10:12-15

Explanation: This is one of the main verses used to fight against Galileo when he was showing evidence that the earth moved around the Sun rather than the sun around the earth. But that is not what this verse is about. When we use the tools of science to examine the passage, we come to the wrong conclusion. Rather, this verse is part of a story whose biggest message is "God fights for God's people." That is an important message for teens who might feel that no one is fighting for them.

Explore: Why do you think the church used this verse to fight against Galileo when he was sharing his scientific observations about the earth moving around the sun? Understanding the bigger message of this verse, that God is fighting for God's people, how does that make the church's fighting against Galileo even more strange? How does it feel to know that God fights for you?

Chapter: Did Genesis really happen? Like, is that how the earth was made?

Scripture: Genesis 2:21-22

Explanation: In the chapter we allowed ourselves to focus on Genesis 1 and divine a deeper message than the more simple, literal one involving God having vocal chords and speaking. We are able to do the same with this verse. When God creates Eve, Adam's rib is used. That isn't just a random choice, it is symbolic of how God desires relationships between people who love each other to be. God didn't create Eve out of a bone of Adam's head so that she would rule over him or a bone from his foot so that he would rule over her. God created her from a rib so that they could go through life as partners side-by-side. Can a student also choose to believe that there was a literal Adam and a literal divine surgical procedure? Sure, but that is not a necessary belief to be able to say that you believe in the truth of Genesis 2.

Explore: What could this part of the story be about other than whether or not God is a good thoracic surgeon? Why a rib? Why not a head bone or a foot bone? Why is it important to explore the symbolism of verses that trouble us? Who is a person in your life who walks with you? How does it feel to find someone that seems to complete you in some way?

Chapter: How can I hold up my faith against science?

Scripture: Psalm 8

Explanation: This chapter ends up talking about God as the creator, and that major theme of the psalm has a lot of depth to mine. In this beautiful poem about God's role as creator the author is ultimately humbled by the fact that the God who created the entire universe cares about humanity. Understanding God's role as creator in this way in no way challenges our ability to also believe in science. It removes the battle lines that have been drawn.

Explore: This poem talks about God as creator. How does that role of God affect the writer? What conclusions are made? What emotions does the writer seem to be feeling? How does viewing God's role as creator in this way free you from the battle between science and faith?

Chapter: What's the deal with dinosaurs?

Scripture: John 21:25

Explanation: This chapter uses a question about dinosaurs as a jumping-off point to discuss questions that the Bible just doesn't answer. And this verse is one of the places in the Bible where the actual text makes it clear that there's stuff that didn't get into the Bible! Not every question is directly answered in the Bible—but we can trust that the Bible tells us everything we need to know about God, and gives us tools to answer a lot of other questions as well.

Explore: What other questions do you have that the Bible doesn't answer? Does the Bible give you any other principles or tools that you can use to approach those questions, even if the actual answer isn't in there? Do you wish the Bible had all the answers, or do you like it that God gives us some important tools and lets us figure some things out for ourselves?

Chapter: How do I know that God hears all of my prayers?

Scripture: Exodus 3:1-10 (especially 7-10)

Explanation: This may seem like an odd scripture for a chapter on prayer. However, what we hear God say through the burning bush relates directly to prayer. In verse 7 God says that he has heard the cries of the people praying to him. The problem is that the people have been enslaved for a long time (possibly hundreds of years). I'm sure that many of those people asked this very same question. But God did hear them and sent Moses as a deliverer.

Explore: Where do you see prayer talked about in this scripture? How do you think it would feel to be a slave crying out to God and not feeling like God was doing anything? God sent Moses as an answer to people's prayers. How can God use you to be an answer to someone else's prayer this week?

Chapter: What about people who claim to be Christians and then do terrible things?

Scripture: James 2:14-17

Explanation: It's hard to know what to do when people who claim to be Christians do terrible things. We know that we are saved by our faith—but in the book of James, we also learn that we demonstrate our faith through what we do. No one but God knows who is really a Christian, so it's dangerous to say with certainty who does and who doesn't have true faith. That's between them and God. However, when someone's bad deeds make all Christians look bad, we can be very clear with others in pointing out that these are not the kind of actions a Christian should be participating in. And, we can demonstrate by our loving deeds the true way that Christians should behave. We don't get to decide who is really part of the body of Christ—and that's a good thing! What we do get to decide is how we act, and the example we set to others by our deeds.

Explore: Talk about a time when you were ashamed by the way that another Christian behaved, either in your life or on the news. Have you ever been the one to act in a way that might make other Christians look bad? How do we forgive our fellow Christians while also making it clear that some actions are not okay? And how can you show the world the true heart of the Christian faith through your deeds?

Chapter: Is it harder to be a Christian if I have ADD?

Scripture: Genesis 1:26-27

Explanation: This chapter ultimately talks about being comfortable with who we are. The theological foundation of that idea comes from understanding this passage in Genesis where it says that we are all created in God's image. No matter if we have ADD or struggle with depression or other tough medical conditions, we are all image bearers of God in this world. Recognizing that we have the image of God is the beginning of real self-esteem, because that is something good that cannot be changed and is in no way dependent on human action or inaction.

Explore: What does it means to have the image of God? How do you see God at work in the world? How does that help you approach the world in a positive way? What does it mean about your role in the world?

Chapter: What does the Bible say about drinking and drugs?

Scripture: 1 Corinthians 6:19-20

Explanation: This chapter talks specifically about drinking and drugs, but there is a bigger discussion to be had around the spirituality of caring for your body. At the most basic level we know that we have been called to do God's work in the world, and that requires us to use our bodies. Taking care of our bodies enables us to do God's work in the world more effectively.

Explore: What does this scripture have to do with drinking and drugs? Why do you think it is spiritually important to take care of our bodies? What kind of practices become spiritual when we understand this verse?

Chapter: Are we supposed to think about God every second of the day? How are we supposed to live like Jesus every day?

Scripture: Colossians 3:1-4

Explanation: This Bible verse is all about the main theme of this chapter: focusing on God. Into that discussion it interjects one of the big themes of the Bible: dying to yourself. Focusing on that connection, what it means, and how it helps us focus on God will help students put practical handles on this abstract topic.

Explore: What do you think is means to "die to yourself?" How does this verse relate that to focusing on God? Make two lists of thoughts: things above and earthly things. How can you think more about the former and less about the latter?